STUDIES IN ECONOMIC AND SOCIAL HISTORY

This series, specially commissioned by the Economic History Society, provides a guide to the current interpretations of the key themes of economic and social history in which advances have recently been made or in which there has been significant debate.

Originally entitled 'Studies in Economic History', in 1974 the series had its scope extended to include topics in social history, and the new series title, 'Studies in Economic and Social History', signalises this development.

The series gives readers access to the best work done, helps them to draw their own conclusions in major fields of study, and by means of the critical bibliography in each book guides them in the selection of further reading. The aim is to provide a springboard to further work rather than a set of pre-packaged conclusions or short-cuts.

ECONOMIC HISTORY SOCIETY

The Economic History Society, which numbers over 3000 members, publishes the *Economic History Review* four times a year (free to members) and holds an annual conference. Enquiries about membership should be addressed to the Assistant Secretary, Economic History Society, Peterhouse, Cambridge. Full-time students may join at special rates.

D0141519

STUDIES IN ECONOMIC AND SOCIAL HISTORY

Edited for the Economic History Society by M. W. Flinn

PUBLISHED

OTHER TITLES ARE IN PREPARATION

CE

Plague, Population and the English Economy 1348–1530

Prepared for
The Economic History Society by

JOHN HATCHER

University Lecturer in History
and Fellow of Corpus Christi
College, Cambridge

Universitas
BIBLIOTHECA
Ottaviensis

© The Economic History Society 1977

All rights reserved. No part of this publication
may be reproduced or transmitted, in any form
or by any means, without permission.

First published 1977 by
THE MACMILLAN PRESS LTD
London and Basingstoke
Associated companies in New York Dublin
Melbourne Johannesburg and Madras

ISBN 0 333 21293 2

Phototypeset by
WESTERN PRINTING SERVICES LTD
Bristol
Printed and bound in Great Britain by
REDWOOD BURN LIMITED
Trowbridge & Esher

This book is sold subject to the standard
conditions of the Net Book Agreement.

The paperback edition of this book is sold subject to the condition
that it shall not, by way of trade or otherwise, be lent, resold,
hired out, or otherwise circulated without the publisher's prior
consent in any form of binding or cover other than that in which
it is published and without a similar condition including this
condition being imposed on the subsequent purchaser.

Contents

Figures

Tables

Acknowledgements

I am indebted to Drs T. H. Hollingsworth, E. Miller and R. S. Schofield for reading a complete draft of the text and making many valuable criticisms; and to Mr A. F. Butcher and Dr R. B. Outhwaite for advice on the passages dealing, respectively, with towns and wages and prices. The faults which remain are, of course, in no respect the responsibility of those who so kindly gave me their advice.

Note on References

References in the text within square brackets relate to the numbered items in the Select Bibliography, followed, where necessary, by the page numbers in italics, for example [131: *207*]. Other references in the text, numbered consecutively throughout the book, relate to annotations of the text or to sources not given in the Select Bibliography, and are itemised in the Notes and References section.

Editor's Preface

S O long as the study of economic and social history was confined to a small group at a few universities, its literature was not prolific and its few specialists had no great problem in keeping abreast of the work of their colleagues. Even in the 1930s there were only two journals devoted exclusively to economic history and none at all to social history. But the high quality of the work of the economic historians during the inter-war period and the post-war growth in the study of the social sciences sparked off an immense expansion in the study of economic history after the Second World War. There was a great expansion of research and many new journals were launched, some specialising in branches of the subject like transport, business or agricultural history. Most significantly, economic history began to be studied as an aspect of history in its own right in schools. As a consequence, the examining boards began to offer papers in economic history at all levels, while textbooks specifically designed for the school market began to be published. As a specialised discipline, social history is an even more recent arrival in the academic curriculum. Like economic history, it, too, is rapidly generating a range of specialist publications. The importance of much of the recent work in this field and its close relationship with economic history have therefore prompted the Economic History Society to extend the scope of this series – formerly confined to economic history – to embrace themes in social history.

For those engaged in research and writing this period of rapid expansion of studies has been an exciting, if rather breathless one. For the larger numbers, however, labouring in the outfield of the schools and colleges of further education, the excitement of the explosion of research has been tempered by frustration arising from its vast quantity and, frequently, its controversial character. Nor, it must be admitted, has the ability or willingness of the academic historians to generalise and summarise marched in step with their enthusiasm for research.

The greatest problems of interpretation and generalisation have tended to gather round a handful of principal themes in economic and social history. It is, indeed, a tribute to the sound sense of economic and social historians that they have continued to dedicate their energies, however inconclusively, to the solution of these key problems. The results of this activity, however, much of it stored away in a wide range of academic journals, have tended to remain inaccessible to many of those currently interested in the subject. Recognising the need for guidance through the burgeoning and confusing literature that has grown around these basic topics, the Economic History Society hopes in this series of short books to offer some help to students and teachers. The books are intended to serve as guides to current interpretations in major fields of economic and social history in which important advances have recently been made, or in which there has recently been some significant debate. Each book aims to survey recent work, to indicate the full scope of the particular problem as it has been opened up by recent scholarship, and to draw such conclusions as seem warranted, given the present state of knowledge and understanding. The authors will often be at pains to point out where, in their view, because of a lack of information or inadequate research, they believe it is premature to attempt to draw firm conclusions. While authors will not hesitate to review recent and older work critically, the books are not intended to serve as vehicles for their own specialist views: the aim is to provide a balanced summary rather than an exposition of the author's own viewpoint. Each book will include a descriptive bibliography.

In this way the series aims to give all those interested in economic and social history at a serious level access to recent scholarship in some major fields. Above all, the aim is to help the reader to draw his own conclusions, and to guide him in the selection of further reading as a means to this end, rather than to present him with a set of pre-packaged conclusions.

M. W. FLINN

University of Edinburgh   *Editor*

1 An Introduction to the Controversy

THE two centuries which followed the Black Death of 1348–9 constitute one of the most intriguing periods in the history of population. In common with other societies in which the great mass of people was employed in agriculture, and in which technical progress was limited, the size of the population of later medieval and early Tudor England was one of the major determinants not only of both aggregate and *per capita* output, but also of the distribution of wealth and the structure of society. Just as the abundance of people prior to 1348 played a major part in reducing the standards of life of the peasantry and strengthening the power of landlords, so the progressive shortage of people in the ensuing era played a major part in undermining demesne agriculture and in bringing about a fundamental redistribution of wealth. The later fourteenth and the fifteenth centuries saw the real wage-rates of craftsmen and labourers apparently reach levels not to be exceeded until the second half of the nineteenth century. These centuries also experienced one of the most decisive shifts ever in social structure and tenurial relationships, namely the decline of serfdom and customary land tenure. But more than this there occurred within these centuries the longest period of declining and stagnant population in recorded English history. The failure of population to rise in a prolonged era of high living standards poses a severe test for many current theories concerning the causality of demographic change. In particular the experience of the late fourteenth and the fifteenth centuries would appear to conflict with the views of a powerful lobby of historians. These historians seek to interpret demographic history in neo-Malthusian terms by arguing that the size of population, and the scale and direction of its movements, were determined primarily by the standard of living and consequent so-called 'homeostatic adjustments' to the age of marriage and the size of families. In so doing they relegate disease to the status

11

of a mere function of the standard of living. For these and other reasons the study of the demography of this era has much to commend it.

More than a generation ago John Saltmarsh and M. M. Postan sketched with bold strokes the profile of English demographic history in the century and a half after the Black Death. Postan at this stage was more concerned with evidence of economic depression than with demography, but he set his analysis firmly in the context of declining population [12]; Saltmarsh was far more explicit and stated that 'the symptoms of the fifteenth century suggest a continuous fall over a long period; not simply a population that had fallen, but one which was falling progressively' [18]. ✓ Their verdict was that after a series of drastic reductions in the third quarter of the fourteenth century population drifted downwards for a century, and few historians chose to disagree. In 1948 J. C. Russell published an extensive study of British population in the Middle Ages [39], based upon a wide range of documentary sources and demographic techniques which, although tentatively dating the commencement of the recovery in numbers from around 1430, at first appeared to lend support and unexpected precision to the thesis of substantial and prolonged decline [39]. Over the next few years Postan, in a series of pioneering studies of the indirect evidence of population movements, used changes in settlement, land values, wages, and prices, to present his case with still greater clarity and conviction [13; 14; 15]. Against such formidable weaponry, now supported by a growing body of sympathetic evidence from Europe, resistance was sparse.[1] A number of critics attempted to resurrect the 'money–price level' thesis, by claiming that a shortage of money rather than population decline was the prime mover behind the falling agricultural prices and general economic recession postulated for the century after 1380, but they did so without directly challenging the basic premise that a substantial long-term fall in the level of population had taken place [127; 129].

This premise was eventually challenged by the distinguished Russian historian, E. A. Kosminsky. In Marxian dialectics the level of population 'cannot be the chief force of development in society', and in a paper published in 1955 Kosminsky claimed that it did not 'appear to be definitely established that there was a fall in population which began in the 1320s and continued until the 1460s or 70s'; he preferred to write instead of 'the temporary fall in population' [8]. Although his resourceful arguments contained many insights and some criticisms of substance, the attempt to explain the major economic and social developments of the later Middle Ages, 'without recourse to the hypothesis of a substantial and long-drawn-out decline in England's population or to "Malthusian" speculations', found little favour with western medievalists and the Postan/Saltmarsh thesis emerged triumphant.[2]

It was perhaps inevitable, given the complexities of the subject and the deficiencies of the sources, that the ever-widening range of data revealed by subsequent studies of the medieval economy and society should have resulted in a retreat from the virtual concord of the 1940s and 50s into something which is now close to discord. Not that many historians have chosen to dispute that a significant fall in numbers occurred or that recovery was somewhat delayed, rather that there is now a distinct lack of agreement about the scale and duration of the decline, and particularly about the population trend after 1377.

One of the major sources of nonconformist beliefs is the work of J. C. Russell. Although first proffered more than a quarter of a century ago, and since subjected to much telling criticism from historians and demographers alike, Russell's speculations on the course of English medieval population continue to command widespread acceptance. Perhaps his most frequently quoted speculation is that the population of England was approximately 3·75 million in 1348, that by 1377 the Black Death and later epidemics had reduced it to 2·2 million, and that thereafter it fell very gently to about 2·1 million in 1400, at which level it remained until around 1430 when a slow recovery commenced [39: 260–81]. It becomes evident from even a brief perusal of *British Medieval Population* that this is an extremely tentative scheme, and one which can be disputed on many grounds. It will suffice to mention only three.

Firstly, there are strong reasons for believing that Russell's estimates of English population in 1348 and 1377 are gross understatements. Since the estimate of 1348 depends upon that derived from the Poll Tax returns of 1377, adjusted to take account of intervening plagues, we shall concentrate upon the latter. (Death-rate during the Black Death and later epidemics is discussed in chapter 2.) The returns of the Poll Tax of 1377, which was levied on all persons over the age of fourteen excepting only genuine indigents, provide the medieval historian with a firm base for calculating the national population. But firm is a relative term and, in common with all medieval statistics, the adjustments and allowances that have to be made in order to transform taxpayers into population are a source of doubt and controversy. None the less, if one makes much more realistic allowances than Russell's derisory 5 per cent for evasion and fraud, for indigents who were legally exempt from taxation, and for the inevitable inefficiences in the collection of this unique tax; and if one corrects a number of lesser imperfections in Russell's calculations, then the total number of taxpayers (1,386,196) can convincingly be transformed into a total population of 2·75–3 million.[3]

Secondly, it is a relatively simple task to demonstrate that Russell's speculations on the post-1377 population trend rest upon extremely shaky foundations. In fact they are based in part upon life-tables, derived not only from medieval but also from twentieth-century Indian sources, and in part upon the numbers of tenants listed in a sample of rural extents and surveys. Of the calculations based upon the former sources, one distinguished demographer has pointed out that 'they are not only afflicted with the uncertainties that beset all statistics but actually contain such curious elements of speculation and guesswork that they must regretfully be dismissed altogether' [38: 70–81]. The dubiety of Russell's use of extents and surveys stems not only from the small size of the sample studied, but also from the artlessness of his methodology. As every agrarian historian knows, the number of tenants holding land directly from the lord of a manor need bear no direct relation to the level of population within that manor, still less to that of a wider area [13: 224; 76: 292]. Finally, and most ironically, Russell's view of the population trend after 1377 conflicts directly with calculations of male generation replacement rates ingeniously made by T. H. Hollingsworth from data that Russell himself collected, but was unable to utilise fully [33: 375–80]. (Replacement rates are discussed below, pp. 26–9.)

Notwithstanding these flaws, the seductive charms of quantification have frequently proved too tempting for historians accustomed to courting cold favours from indirect evidence, and Russell's speculations, through widespread acceptance and repetition, have at times come perilously close to achieving the status of orthodoxy. In the last few years his estimates of national population have been described as 'the best available statistics of population' in medieval Europe [11: *19*] and they have provided the data for the medieval sections of numerous graphs of long-term population change, including those constructed by such notable historical demographers as J. D. Chambers [23: *19*] and E. A. Wrigley [43: *78*].

It is clear then that those who would see the era of severe population fall drawing to an end by the late 1370s are by no means mere uncritical supporters of the views of Russell. On the contrary a substantial body of influential opinion now rejects the possibility that numbers decreased significantly in the course of the fifteenth century. G. Duby, in his masterly survey of the rural economy of western Europe, declares that, 'Everything leads us to believe that the real fall in the rural population occurred between 1350 and 1380', and 'that the following sixty years was a period of stagnation interrupted only intermittently by catastrophes' [67: *308–10*]. A. R. Bridbury, in his controversial attempt to demonstrate economic growth in late medieval England, assumes that demographic recession was primarily confined to the period between 1348 and 1369, after which 'the shock was over . . . population began to adapt itself' [2: *23*]; an opinion shared by H. A. Miskimin [123: *479*] and J. Schreiner [129: *71–2*].

J. M. W. Bean's study of the habits, incidence and impact of plague in late medieval England has been most effectual in forming and marshalling opinion against the thesis of continued population decline. Indeed his article published in 1963 has strong claims to be counted among the most influential to be written on English late medieval demography since 1950 [1]. Starting out to test Saltmarsh's conclusion that the evidence of the fifteenth century suggests 'not simply a population that had fallen, but one which was falling progressively' [18: *30*], Bean ended by claiming that 'it seems likely that the decline of the population of England had been arrested by the end of the fourteenth century and that some expansion then ensued' [1: *435*].

The growing band of historians seeking to interpret the fifteenth century as an era of prosperity and enterprise have found the hypothesis of population increase most appealing. The fearsome spectre of recurrent plague, swingeing mortality rates, and a morbid preoccupation with death, are not readily compatible with an age of vitality. F. R. H. Du Boulay, while not concerned in detail with demographic matters, writes that, 'Studies on the effects of plague have progressed from J. Saltmarsh . . . to J. M. W.

15

Bean', and maintains that although, 'it was once thought that the death-rate from the plague was continuous enough to bring down the population without remission from 1348 until late in the fifteenth century . . . there were in fact long gaps between outbreaks which, together with their less lethal incidence, allowed momentary rises in the birth-rate' [5: *34, 182*]. Professor Lander is even more confident and concludes that, 'Everything argues against any continuous decline or even stagnation of the population', and that a slow but progressive recovery in numbers was under way by 1430 [9: *35, 46–7*].

Close examination reveals, however, that the case of those who would argue that the decline in numbers was over by 1370 or 1380, and that some measure of sustained recovery was accomplished in the ensuing century, rests not upon positive evidence of demographic vitality but upon the negative argument that fifteenth-century outbreaks of plague were neither so general, so frequent, nor so virulent as to have been able to restrain the powerful forces of recovery, still less to have effected a further significant decline. As expressed by its foremost proponent, J. M. W. Bean, this case has a number of serious flaws. In the first place it relies almost exclusively upon chronicles for evidence of plague outbreaks. Bean himself states: 'For our knowledge of the chronology of plague in England during the later Middle Ages we must rely almost completely on the evidence of contemporary chronicles, supplemented by the reference made occasionally in government records' [1: *427*]. Since he relies so heavily upon this source it is strange to find that no space is given to a discussion of possible changes in its quality. Chroniclers are not uniformly informative and those of the fourteenth and very early fifteenth centuries were far more likely to have recorded national outbreaks of plague than were those of later years. By the first quarter of the fifteenth century the tradition established by such as Walsingham, Knighton, Higden, Adam of Usk, and the *Anonimalle Chronicle* was near extinction; the national chronicler was largely superseded by the local, who paid more attention to the affairs of the house or town to which he belonged than to those of the nation. C. Creighton, the first investigator to use chronicles systematically for evidence of plague, was well aware of the marked deterioration in quality which had taken place by the opening decades of the fifteenth century, and writes of 'the not very complete records of the time' [47: *229, 232–3*]; and the views of the majority of historians are summarised by a recent commentator who writes of chronicles, 'As we move into the fifteenth century abundance is replaced by real dearth' [134: 16–17].

Secondly, a major part of Bean's case appears to rest on the assumption that, in order to have had a significant effect on the level of population, plague had to strike through national outbreaks. Thus he maintains that the twenty-one-year gap that he finds between the 'national' plagues of 1413 and 1434 and the twenty-five-year gap between those of 1439 and 1464 'must have enabled a considerable recovery of population level to occur'. But is it correct to concentrate solely or even primarily on national outbreaks at the expense of local? Can it be assumed that all the national outbreaks have been identified or that periodic epidemics of local or regional scale were of little significance in determining the level of population? There can be no doubt that a thorough search of local records will reveal a multitude of explicit references to additional outbreaks of plague and other diseases, while many more may be traced through fluctuations in the numbers of heriots, wills presented for probate, and institutions of priests to benefices.

Valuable testimony to the frequency and virulence of fifteenth-century plagues is provided by the unique obituary lists of Christ Church Priory, Canterbury, which contain details of deaths in a community of seventy-five to eighty-five monks, including special notes on most of those who succumbed to plague [22; 139]. Between 1413 and 1507 plague visited the priory at least once in every decade, saving only the 1490s (namely 1413, 1419, 1420, 1431, 1447, 1457, 1465, 1467, 1470, 1471, 1487, 1501, 1504 and 1507), and accounted for a minimum of 16 per cent of all deaths (i.e. 41 out of a total of 254 deaths).[4] It must be stressed that this is an absolute minimum figure, since in some parts of the lists the recording of deaths is extremely brief and some plague victims may have escaped record. As to the relative impact of 'national' and 'local' plagues the evidence is striking: of the fourteen years in which plague was recorded at Christ Church only four coincided with outbreaks which have hitherto been deemed national (namely 1413, 1465, 1467 and 1471); these 'national' outbreaks accounted for little more than one-fifth of all plague deaths; and more than half of all recorded plague deaths at Christ Church occurred in the two periods (1414–33 and 1440–63) declared by Bean to be free of national plagues. As we shall see later (pp. 57–8) there are grounds for believing that the number of national or extra-regional plagues has been underestimated; at least a further four outbreaks of plague at the priory (in 1420, 1431, 1457 and 1487) occurred in years for which outbreaks have been identified elsewhere in the country. Plague was not the only epidemic disease to strike the priory: three monks died in the autumn of 1435 *ex epidemia*, and an outbreak of 'sweat' in 1485 killed nine monks in the space of six days. Moreover, if we turn to the records of the city of Canterbury, we can identify at least three additional major outbreaks of epidemic disease within our period. The counting of 'national' epidemics clearly constitutes a most unsatisfactory index of mortality.

Finally, another plank in Bean's case can be shown to be insecure, namely that fifteenth-century plagues were mild because they had little immediate impact on the amounts of cloth exported from London [1:433–4]. The significance that Bean claims for the fact that in only one of eleven London plague years between 1407 and 1479 were cloth exports below the totals of both the preceding and the succeeding year, is rendered questionable by the fact that on the terms of this definition neither the notorious *pestis secunda* of 1361 nor the *pestis tertia* of 1368 could be counted as severe plagues.[5] Not only were cloth exports in these later fourteenth-century plague years not below the totals of both the preceding and succeeding years, they actually exceeded the average of the two preceding and two succeeding years.[6] Yet no one can doubt the virulence of these outbreaks, and we know that London was sorely afflicted by them. It is clearly dubious to attempt to measure the virulence of plague by the level of cloth exports.

The most extreme assessment to date of the incidence of plague in late medieval England was made in 1970 by J. F. D. Shrewsbury [53]. By a relentless application of hypothesis based upon a personal interpretation of the aetiology of plague, Shrewsbury denies both that England became an enzootic area in the later Middle Ages and that pneumonic plague was of more than scant significance.* He also asserts that bubonic outbreaks were

*Pneumonic plague is spread by droplet infection, in a fashion which has some similarity with the common cold or influenza; bubonic plague normally can be transmitted only through the bite of an infected flea. In addition to its greater propensity to spread rapidly, pneumonic plague has an even higher mortality rate

unlikely to have been either frequent or severe in rural areas owing to the low density of both rat and human populations. In this way Shrewsbury is able to conclude that in all probability the national death-roll from the Black Death itself did not exceed 5 per cent, and that the vast bulk of the pestilences identified in the late fourteenth and the fifteenth centuries were not plague but other epidemic diseases, among which typhus is his favourite choice. Although he chooses not to concern himself with questions of the general course of population change, the conclusion we are invited to draw from Shrewsbury's work is similar to that to be drawn from Bean's – namely that plague could not have caused a prolonged decline in England's population. It would be out of place to conduct here a detailed refutation of Shrewsbury's analysis since this has been attempted by others, with respect both to his neglect of the major sources of historical evidence which have come to light since the 1930s, and to certain of his opinions concerning the aetiology of plague. Nevertheless it should be noted that immediate reactions to his analysis of the impact of late medieval plague have not all been condemnatory, and some historians are in danger of finding the mixture of Shrewsbury and Bean an intoxicating brew.[7]

Thus, although scarcely any positive evidence of population increase before the latter part of the fifteenth century has so far been forthcoming, the thesis of prolonged decline has been gravely weakened by increasing scepticism and the lack of recent detailed exposition. Indeed in the twenty-five years or so since the pioneering articles of Saltmarsh and Postan scarcely any attempt has been made to incorporate subsequent research into a thorough restatement, despite the fact that the bulk of the studies that have been written on particular aspects of late medieval economy and society have either produced evidence of low or falling population or been placed in a context which assumes such a process. Small wonder then that E. A. Wrigley should feel so bemused when surveying the demographic history of a period well outside his normal purview, that he should write on p. 77 of *Population and History* that after the Black Death, 'There then followed a very interesting period lasting perhaps a century and a quarter during which population, though now much smaller in

– 99·99 per cent compared with 60–85 per cent for bubonic. An enzootic area is one in which some rats at any given moment are infected with plague; successive outbreaks do not therefore have to rely upon fresh importations of infected rats.

size than in the late thirteenth century, seems not to have shown any clear tendency to rise', and then on p. 78 present a graph entitled, 'Long-term Population Trends in England and Wales, 1000 to 1800', which shows population rising quite sharply from around 1430; or that J. Cornwall should write in 1970 of 'our virtually complete ignorance of fifteenth-century demography' [24: 42].

In fact a substantial range of direct and indirect evidence is in existence and, although it is likely that controversies over the demographic history of the later Middle Ages will rage for many years to come, this evidence enables the limits of our ignorance to be charted with some confidence.

2   Direct Evidence of Population Change

HISTORICAL demography, a difficult pursuit in any age, is especially daunting in the English Middle Ages, a period with no parish registers, no hearth-taxes, no large-scale censuses excepting Domesday Book, and few serviceable taxation returns excepting those of 1377. Direct demographic evidence is not only sparse, it is also highly selective, and relates primarily to the mortality of the wealthy and privileged groups in society. It is most unlikely that any adequate data on birth-rates will ever be forthcoming from English sources. Nevertheless it would be displaying not only an unwarranted pessimism but also a culpable ignorance of the sophistication of modern demographic techniques to assume that no worthwhile vital statistics can be extracted from surviving records.

(i) MORTALITY IN THE BLACK DEATH AND SUBSEQUENT EPIDEMICS

The first and also the most devastating visitation of plague, the 'Great Pestilence' or 'Black Death' of 1348–9, has understandably exerted a fascination over successive generations of scholars, many of whom have participated in the perennially intriguing task of attempting to gauge the death-rate of that horrendous event. Precision still proves elusive, but over the years substantial advances in knowledge and technique have enabled us to proceed far beyond the overwrought imaginings and hopelessly inaccurate quantification of the chroniclers, to a position where the majority of historians are agreed upon a reasonably narrow range of probabilities.

Among the most accurate calculations that can be made, and also among the most widely based, are those of the death-rates of the beneficed clergy. Bishops' registers contain records of the institutions of priests to benefices, and the most detailed of these registers enable vacancies caused by deaths to be distinguished

21

from vacancies caused by resignations or exchanges. Careful calculations based upon the registers of the dioceses of Lichfield, York, and Lincoln, which are thought to be the most informative of all, yield death-rates of around 40 per cent for the year of the plague. Less informative registers, of which seven have been analysed, produce maximum death-rates of around 45 per cent. Since each diocese covered more than one county these registers provide a useful guide to the mortality of the beneficed clergy over a large part of England [33: 232–5; 39: 220–2]. Further, though much less significant, measures of clerical mortality are provided by average death-rates of 45 per cent in a dozen monastic houses, and of 18 per cent among bishops and 42 per cent among abbots [39: 221–6; 132: 495–6]. Another measure of mortality can be derived from the experience of tenants-in-chief, whose deaths and successions are recorded in a range of documents called Inquisitions *Post Mortem*. Of a sample of 505 such persons who were in possession of their inheritances in 1348, 138 or just over 27 per cent died in the year of the plague [39: 215–18].

For an indication of the mortality of the population at large we can turn to manorial records. One method of calculating rural death-rates is from the numbers of landholdings which fell vacant during the plague year. A good series of manorial records will enable deaths to be established with a fair degree of accuracy from the payment of death-duties called heriots, and these can be compared with the number of holdings on the manor liable to render heriots on the deaths of their tenants. Sadly the disruption caused by the plague often resulted in the keeping of very imperfect records during the height of the epidemic, and in addition to good account and court rolls an accurate calculation depends upon the availability of a list of landholdings made just prior to the plague. Despite the difficulties a number of calculations have been made, of varying degrees of trustworthiness, which generally suggest very high death-rates. For example it is suggested that two-thirds of the customary tenantry of the manors of Bishop's Waltham, Hants [20: 69–70], Downton, Wilts., and Witney [83: 196,213]) and Cuxham, Oxon., died [75: 135–6]; between 50 and 60 per cent of those of three Cambridgeshire manors [85: 120–5], two Essex manors [48: 13–20], and two east-Cornish manors [76: 102–5]; and a third of those of the manor of Brightwell in Berkshire [83: 207–8]. Other calculations, based upon the decline in the numbers of persons paying customary dues just before and just after the plague, suggest average death-rates of 55 per cent on twenty-two Glastonbury Abbey manors and 43 per cent on three Essex manors [20: *70–1*; 39: *226–7*].

It is particularly frustrating that the most widely based data, and probably also the most accurate, relate not to the mass of the people but to the beneficed clergy, while the data relating to the peasantry are extremely sparse. Accordingly it can readily be appreciated that the task of converting these variable and scattered statistics into a death-rate for the whole English population is fraught with formidable difficulties. Beginning with our mortality rates for parish priests, there are numerous problems involved in calculating a precise death-rate from records of institutions. One has to be especially careful to eliminate all vacancies excepting those arising from death; in plague years the number of resignations rose sharply [132: *498–9*]. One must also take account of the interval between the death of an incumbent and the institution of his successor (this appears to have been at least one month); failure to allow for this interval will have the effect of reducing the population at risk and therefore artificially reducing the death-rate. Pluralities and absenteeism are also complicating factors. If we are satisfied with the accuracy of our calculations, we have to attempt to assess the relationship the mortality of priests bore to that of the common people. The fact that priests were on average better fed, better housed and better educated would have tended to lower death-rates, but the conscientious performance of pastoral duties would have tended to raise them. The high average age of the beneficed clergy would have led to a high 'normal' death-rate.

The 27 per cent death-rate calculated for major landholders is clearly out of line with that suggested for the beneficed clergy and the peasantry. There can be little doubt that this privileged group had a greater than average chance of escaping infection; they lived in stone houses not favoured by rats, and being more mobile than the peasantry they could flee before the advancing plague. But perhaps the most serious doubts on the representative nature of death-rates drawn from Inquisitions *Post Mortem* are aroused by the small size of the sample population at risk, which was a mere 505. These doubts are confirmed by the suggestion that no less than 23 per cent of heirs and heiresses died in the next plague of 1361–2, an outbreak which all other sources of evidence – literary, manorial and clerical, quantitative and qualitative – agree was far less virulent than the Black Death. The implication must be that the samples are too small to produce reliable figures for individual years.

Looking closely at the death-rates calculated from manorial sources, the likelihood is that they are at times somewhat exaggerated. In particular it is probable that on some manors two or even more heriots may have been received from the same holdings, since some of those who inherited may also have died. This would have the effect of artificially inflating the number of deaths in the original population at risk and, if it is not eliminated, of exaggerating the resulting death-rates. As for the statistics derived from customary payments, these are almost certainly over-estimates, since dead men could not continue to pay but live men could take the opportunity presented by the plague to evade payment.

The steady increase in our knowledge means that we can now begin to answer the crucial question of whether the impact of the plague was approximately uniform throughout the country, or whether some regions escaped almost unscathed. Despite the plausibility of arguments based upon scattered settlement and the consequent obstacles to the transmission of disease, it would appear that there is no reason to believe that as a rule the plague claimed fewer victims in the more remote parts of the country. Contemporaries attest that the plague spread throughout the kingdom with unabated ferocity; local studies suggest the death-rates in the Highland zone were as high as those in the more densely settled regions of lowland England; and bishops' registers suggest death-rates for the beneficed clergy of over 50 per cent in the far south-west and 48 per cent in Herefordshire [53: 56]. There would, therefore, seem to be no justification for striking a lower national average on these grounds. A further difficulty in our attempt to arrive at a national estimate stems from the fact that none of our sources provides adequate evidence of death-rates among children and adolescents, relating almost exclusively to office-holders and tenants who, in the vast majority of cases, were adults. There is some evidence from the chronicles that the first outbreak of plague, unlike many of those to follow, struck mainly at people in the prime of life, but in all honesty we must admit that this is yet another area of doubt. We must also appreciate that we have no reliable information on urban death-rates, but we know that both in the nature of bubonic plague and according to the testimony of contemporaries, the proportion dying in towns was likely to have significantly exceeded that dying in the countryside [43: 95–7].

In some respects the range of estimates of the national death-toll espoused by historians might still be considered depressingly wide. Some historians press for a half or even more, others seek refuge in the now conventional estimate of a third and, as we have already mentioned, Shrewsbury would have the proportion of plague victims as low as one-twentieth outside East Anglia [53: 36, 123]. Thus the elements of doubt and confusion in the evidence are reflected in the views of historians. Yet step by step the range of possibilities can be reduced. A national death-rate of below 25 per cent or above 55 per cent would appear most unlikely. In addition to the data rehearsed above there are literally hundreds of mid-fourteenth-century records of manors, towns and other communities throughout the country which bear testimony, with a lack of precision but a compelling force, to a death-rate of at least 30 to 35 per cent; yet when we look at England in the 1350s a death-rate of more than a half would not appear to be compatible with the progress of the economy and the behaviour of prices and wages (see pp. 47–52 below). Until more evidence of rural death-rates is forthcoming great weight must be attached to a revised average death-rate of around 35 to 40 per cent for beneficed clergy. In fact it is fitting that it should provide the mid-point of the most judicious estimate of the national death-rate in 1348–9 in the present state of knowledge: 30 to 45 per cent.[8]

Information on the toll of ensuing epidemics is far less satisfactory. For 1361–2 we have the 23 per cent for heirs and heiresses mentioned earlier, and 14 per cent for beneficed clergy in the diocese of York. For 1369 the rate for heirs and heiresses falls to 13 per cent, and the same figure is recorded for the beneficed clergy of York Diocese [39: 217–18, 222]. For the fourth major national outbreak of 1375, and for outbreaks thereafter, we have as yet no reliable statistical evidence whatsoever.

In assessing the incidence of plague we must not neglect a most valuable index compiled by Russell from Inquisitions *Post Mortem*, namely the time of year at which tenants-in-chief died [39: 195–9]. Russell's findings demonstrate a remarkable transformation in the seasonal pattern of mortality in the century after 1348, and provide a strong indication that this transformation was caused by the virulence of bubonic plague and other summer diseases. The pre-Black Death pattern with, as one would expect, the heaviest mortality in the winter months was succeeded by one in which the heaviest mortality was concentrated in the period from late July to late September. Furthermore Russell found that as the pattern in the years after 1348 which did not experience large-scale epidemics was also markedly different from that in the pre-plague period it was likely that plague had become endemic. The samples upon which these findings are based are of necessity modest, but once again there is ample scope to enlarge them by using evidence contained in wills and bishops' registers.

(ii) REPLACEMENT RATES

Even for a period which was afflicted repeatedly by virulent epidemics on a national and local scale, estimates of the incidence of disease can provide only an imperfect guide to fluctuations in the size of the nation's population. Knowledge of mortality needs to be supplemented by knowledge of fertility. In this respect one of the most promising avenues of investigation to be opened up in recent years is the calculation of generation replacement rates: that is the number of children, usually male, surviving the death of one or other of the parents, usually the father. Replacement rates are, of course, not a perfect substitute for birth-rates, and may at times tell us more about infant and childhood mortality than about birth, but since they are the closest the medievalist is ever likely to get to birth-rates they are too valuable to spurn. By far the best series of replacement rates is that calculated by T. H. Hollingsworth from the data extracted by Russell from Inquisitions *Post Mortem* [33: 375–80]. On the death of a tenant-in-chief an inquest was held to determine, *inter alia*, the heir to the landholdings. The report of the inquest could take three forms: first, a statement concerning the sole or eldest son, or his heir or heirs; second, if there were no sons, a list of all surviving daughters; third, a statement that there were no direct heirs. Thus if there were at least one son the inquest did not have to report how many sons there actually were, but fortunately if there were no sons the report had to list all the daughters. Using an ingenious method, Hollingsworth has managed to calculate male generation replacement rates by allocating sons on the basis of the data concerning daughters. It must be readily admitted that the results of these calculations are speculative, but Inquisitions *Post Mortem* are among the most trustworthy of extant sources for information concerning heirs. Furthermore, even if there are doubts concerning the precise orders of magnitude, the relative changes are significant, and the samples upon which they are based are large enough and the results consistent enough to warrant serious consideration.

Table I

Male Generation Replacement Rates Calculated from Inquisitions *Post Mortem*

Period	Deaths	Sons Calculated	Replacement Rate
Up to 1265	347	568	1·64
1266–90	568	718	1·26
1291–1315	1043	1335	1·28
1316–40	1093	1535	1·40
1341–65	1348	1332	0·99
1366–90	761	619	0·81
1391–1415	696	558	0·80
1416–40	769	628	0·82
1441–65	631	695	1·10
1466–90	887	1076	1·21
1491–1505	673	1359	2·02

SOURCES: Russell [39: *240–2*]; Hollingsworth [33: *375–80*].

NOTE: When assessing the value of these data the following factors should be borne in mind: (1) uncertainty as to the precise point in time to which each replacement rate refers; (2) the rates do not fully reflect the effects of crisis mortality years when a series of deaths might occur in the same family in a very short space of time; (3) children conceived but not born at the time of death of the father are not recorded; (4) some of the recorded sons would not survive into adulthood; (5) daughters who had entered nunneries were not recorded.

It will be noted that not a single positive replacement occurs in any twenty-five-year period between 1341 and 1440, while even if five-year periods are used only one positive replacement occurs, namely 1386–90 (1·14). If these replacement rates were applied to the nation as a whole, the population of England would have fallen with virtually no remission for a century, at a rate which Hollingsworth estimates would have totalled 50 per cent; and almost 20 per cent of the decline would have occurred after 1377. But clearly they are not readily applicable. Tenants-in-chief were a small and highly favoured section of society, and their living standards were far in excess of those of the mass of people; on the other hand they were perhaps more likely than the population at large to suffer violent deaths in the frequent hostilities of the times. Weighing all the factors, Hollingsworth has estimated on the basis of the replacement rate evidence that England's population as a whole may well have declined by around two-thirds in the century after the Black Death [33: 380–8].

The imaginative attempt by Professor Thrupp to coax accurate replacement rates from manorial court rolls must be deemed to have failed; sadly so because direct evidence of the demographic history of the peasantry is almost wholly lacking [40]. Even long series of detailed manorial court records are capable of yielding a far less comprehensive and accurate picture of the life of medieval rural communities than many present researchers would wish. On the death of a customary tenant who held by impartible tenure there was necessity to record only the direct heir, while even the entail of a partible inheritance resulted only in the listing of sons already of age. To believe that all or even most of the extra sons ineligible to inherit will be able to be traced in other proceedings of the court is surely to be unrealistically optimistic. Even if difficulties over the inconsistent use of surnames are discounted, it must be admitted that the deficiencies of the rolls themselves did not remain constant. In the fifteenth century even the most efficiently administered manors witnessed some deterioration in the standard of management, and villagers for their part were less likely than their predecessors of the thirteenth century to welcome the opportunity of inheriting a customary holding, and some no doubt took positive steps to avoid having to inherit. Furthermore, it was inevitable that the information available to the court was often imperfect, and the incentive for court officials to be diligent was frequently lacking. These and other inevitable sources of 'leakage' mean that the number of sons that can be identified must almost invariably be an understatement.[9]

S. Thrupp's pioneering method of using sons named as beneficiaries in wills as a means of calculating male replacement rates probably produces more useful results, and in so far as the factors making for the under-enumeration of sons in wills may well be more constant than in court rolls the trend may well have some significance [40: 114–18]. In fact the replacement rates calculated from both court rolls and wills follow a trend similar to that followed by replacement rates calculated from Inquisitions *Post Mortem*. The rates from court rolls fall sharply between the later thirteenth century and the mid-fifteenth, while those from fifteenth-century wills remain well below unity until the closing decades of the century. But it comes as no surprise that the rates themselves are unrealistically low. Indeed it has been computed that the rates calculated by Thrupp would have produced a fall of about 60 per cent per generation in the century or so after the Black Death, with the result that, on the basis of 2·2 million in 1377, the population of England by about 1470 would have stood at an incredible 142,000! [33: 222–3].

Notwithstanding, S. Thrupp has taught us that manorial court rolls should not be discarded for together with wills they can almost certainly be made to yield valuable demographic data. An examination of succession to partible patrimonies based upon excellent series of court rolls has potentially rewarding possibilities, and the use of wills in great numbers, using beneficiaries to calculate replacement rates, is a promising avenue of investigation.

Finally, in passing, attention should be drawn to the direct demographic evidence which can be derived from the obituary book and ordination lists of Christ Church Priory, Canterbury [22; 139]. The full and continuous recording of both ordinations and deaths at the priory between 1394 and 1504 permit the calculation not only of crude death-rates, but also of the size and age-structure of the monastic population, and hence of life-tables. Inevitably there are shortcomings, not least the small size of the population at risk (generally between seventy-five and eighty-five monks), and the fact that it was not representative of the population at large. Many difficult methodological problems need to be solved before the Christ Church data can be presented in the most accurate and informative manner, but preliminary analysis reveals high and fluctuating levels of mortality in the priory.[10]

Turning first to the simplest of calculations, crude death-rates, we find that they range from as low as the mid-twenties per thousand in the healthiest decades to as high as the mid-forties per thousand in the unhealthiest. Over the 110-year period covered they averaged more than thirty per thousand. Not only are such levels high, the wide fluctuations they exhibit are characteristic of a community experiencing waves of epidemic disease, an observation borne out by the information contained in the obituary book of time and cause of death. These rates were not unduly influenced by changes in the age-structure of the monastic population, since the average age of the community varied between the relatively narrow limits of the mid-30s to early 40s, and tended to drop in times of high mortality as new monks were ordained to take the places of those who died. During the course of the fifteenth century Christ Church monks were ordained at an average age of 17 to 19 years, and died at an average age of somewhat less than 50 years.

Comparative data are hard to come by, but it is significant that a preliminary attempt to construct a life-table for the cohort of just under 80 monks who were ordained between 1395 and 1423 produces expectations of life that are, age for age, as low as, or even lower than, those calculated for men and women at an average age of 25 years during the 'worst period' at Colyton, between 1625 and 1699 when there was a surplus of burials over baptisms and 'population was apparently falling' [45]; farmers in Crulai at an average age of 27 in the 'crisis' period of 1675 to 1742 [26: *176 ff.*]; and male members of the British peerage aged 20 years at any time from the beginning of calculations in 1550 [32: *56*]. Moreover, the incidence of death did not follow an orderly progression according to advancing years; in fact the mortality level of the 25–34 years age-group was frequently in excess of that of the 35–44 years age-group, and sometimes even in excess of that of the 45–54 years age-group. If such a characteristic obtained in England at large it would have severely restricted the growth potential of the population. Indeed even if no allowance is made for the abundant food of excellent quality and the impressive standards of hygiene and medical care enjoyed by the monks, the Christ Church data provide still further evidence that the population of England declined throughout much of the fifteenth century.

3 Economic Evidence of Population Change

THE study of the demographic history of the Middle Ages provides confirmation of the aphorism that 'necessity is the mother of invention'. Faced with scarce and imperfect sources of direct evidence of population medieval historians have ingeniously sought to utilise a wide range of indirect evidence, including prices and wages, the occupation and value of land, and the prosperity of the urban and industrial sectors. Yet indirect evidence, by its very nature, is imprecise and difficult to interpret and consequently extreme care must be exercised in its use. A striking instance of the need for caution is provided by the experience of the later fourteenth century.

(i) THE LATER FOURTEENTH-CENTURY ECONOMY

There are many aspects of the economic and social history of the later fourteenth century which remain extremely puzzling, and the formulation of satisfactory explanations will occupy historians for many generations to come. In the first place the Black Death and the immediately ensuing waves of devastating epidemics which, as far as it is possible to judge at present, must have led to a reduction in population of at least a third and more probably almost a half, had few of the debilitating effects that one has been led to associate with the population decline of the later Middle Ages. Indeed the often quoted epithet 'depression' fits the facts of the fifteenth century far better than those of the later fourteenth, while 'economic growth' can justifiably be applied to the later fourteenth century but not to the fifteenth. A remarkable buoyancy in agriculture was emulated by the fortunes of many towns and many branches of industry and commerce. The immense loss of life in the plagues inevitably caused disruption and setbacks in production, but in greater part these appear to have been short-lived.

31

One of the most striking features of the thirty and more years following 1348 was the resilience that the agrarian economy displayed in the face of recurrent plague. Although blows had been struck at the prosperity of 'high farming' at least as early as the second decade of the fourteenth century, blows which were redoubled in 1348–9, 1360–2 and 1368–9, the era refused to be brought to a summary demise, and by the end of the third quarter of the century large numbers of landlords, perhaps even the majority, were enjoying revenues not decisively below those received in pre-plague years. Naturally the precise timing of the post-Black Death recovery and its extent and composition varied from estate to estate and from region to region, but with a few exceptions a peak of seigneurial prosperity was reached before many years of the fifteenth century had elapsed.

The most frequently quoted illustration of this phenomenon is the fortunes of certain estates of the higher nobility situated in East Anglia, Denbigh, Monmouthshire, Somerset and Dorset, whose yields in the 1370s were found by G. A. Holmes to have been less than 10 per cent below those of the 1340s [79: *ch. 4*]. Yet many other equally striking examples can be given, and many more doubtless remain to be discovered. The vast and widely scattered estates of the Duchy of Lancaster, still to be studied in their entirety, provide much complementary evidence; from the Honour of Tutbury's estates in Staffordshire and Derbyshire, for example, we learn of the re-leasing of many previously vacant tenements in the 1360s and 70s, and of rent receipts from a group of manors which in the same period were no more than 10 per cent lower than in 1313 [57: *74–81*]. Ecclesiastical estates, as we might expect, enjoyed fortunes no less propitious than these, and we learn that the manorial revenues of the bishopric of Winchester in the later fourteenth century 'remained remarkably (though also precariously) high' [16: *588–9*]; that the estates of Ramsey Abbey enjoyed an 'economic recovery [in] the 1370s and 1380s' [88: *259–65*]; that the first signs of difficulty in securing tenants for vacant holdings on Crowland Abbey estates were encountered as late as 1391 [85: *152–3*]; and that the income of Christ Church Priory, Canterbury, reached 'its highest recorded level' in 1411 [93: *194*]. Even more impressive evidence of buoyant demand for land is forthcoming from both ecclesiastical and lay estates in south-western counties [70: *253–7*; 76: *ch. 6*].

Late medieval England was a predominantly peasant economy, and with perhaps three-quarters of the population consisting of peasant farmers and farm labourers, and a relatively static technology, changes in the level of population ought to have been reflected in the competition for land, and particularly in the amount of land under cultivation and the value placed upon it. The tell-tale signs of a low or falling population are consequently vacant holdings, arable reverting to rough pasture, low or falling rents and entry fines, the accumulation of rent arrears and so on. The historian's dilemma regarding the later fourteenth century is that none of these things appear to have happened on a scale commensurate with a population decline of around 35 to 50 per cent. At present the most plausible resolution of this dilemma appears to lie in overpopulation before 1348 and a marked increase in *per capita* output and income afterwards, which combined to offset the characteristically depressive effects of the decline in absolute numbers. In the case of agriculture increased costs in the form of wages and equipment may have been balanced by the fact that prices for farm produce in the thirty years after the Black Death were maintained at very high levels, and output per acre may well have risen. (For wage and price data, see below pp. 47–54.)

There are many good reasons why the reduction in population should have led to a rise in *per capita* output. It is now generally agreed that England, along with many parts of Europe, was suffering from some degree of overpopulation in the early fourteenth century, and that diminishing returns had long since begun to operate in many sectors of the economy. There is widespread evidence of the cultivation of poor soils at this time, of holdings far below the optimum size, and of an abundance of labour which inevitably produced chronic under- and unemployment. The subsequent reduction in population must have led to increased productivity by restoring a more efficient balance between labour, land and capital. The reduction in population must also have led to a sharp increase in *per capita* wealth and consumption. In simple terms, the survivors inherited the property of those who had perished and, when presented with a sudden increase in wealth at a time of recurrent plague and considerable uncertainty, it is not surprising that they chose to spend on a greater scale than their predecessors. Demand was further stimulated by the increasing earnings of labourers and peasants; and there is also the possibility that these groups had a greater propensity to consume than landlords and others who suffered a relative reduction in income. The 'outrageous and excessive' expenditure of the lower and middle classes was one of the favourite themes of the moralists of the age, and we can take as representative the sentiments of Henry Knighton, a canon of Leicester, who wrote in 1388 of 'the elation of the inferior people in dress and accoutrements in these days, so that one person cannot be discerned from another in splendour of dress or belongings, neither poor from rich nor servant from master' [5: 67]. With the trappings of the cherished hierarchy of status under such determined assault Parliament attempted, with a series of notably unsuccessful sumptuary statutes beginning in 1363, to restrain conspicuous expenditure and regulate personal possessions according to occupation and income [123: 486–90; 130].

The urban sector was inevitably a prime beneficiary of this increase in *per capita* consumption. For large numbers of towns the early fourteenth century brought the onset of difficult trading conditions, and for a time the Black Death seemed likely to precipitate a major long-term crisis. Yet within a decade or so of the first plague many towns, particularly the larger centres, were showing signs of strong recovery. Some well-known examples of revived fortunes or new growth in the late fourteenth century include York, Newcastle, Norwich, Boston, Lynn, Coventry, Southampton and Bristol, and doubtless many more will be found to add to this list.[11] Evidence of the output and trade of individual commodities is limited but none the less highly suggestive. The development of the English woollen textile industry is a remarkable instance of rapid growth in the face of rapid population decline. The average annual exports of English woollens rose from less than 2000 cloths in the early 1350s to over 40,000 cloths between 1390 and 1395, while the number of cloths supplied to the home market may well have doubled. Although this industrial development inevitably reduced the exports of raw wool, in terms of both weight of wool and value, combined exports of raw wool and cloth reached a peak in the last decade of the fourteenth century comparable with previous peaks in the first and sixth decades.[12] The production of tin, also a leading export commodity, used primarily in the manufacture of pewter, followed an upward path similar to that of cloth. The effect of the Black Death on tin output was little short of catastrophic, but after many setbacks production had risen by the late 1380s to levels barely below the highest hitherto recorded [106: *155–9*]. Further quantitative evidence of economic resilience comes from wine imports, albeit greatly influenced by the current state of hostilities in the Hundred Years War, which suggest that the turn of the century saw a return to prosperity in the wine trade with demand, as also in the case of tin, seemingly not greatly affected by steep increases in price [109: *30–4*].

(ii) THE FIFTEENTH-CENTURY ECONOMY

These propitious times were not to persist, however, and at some point in the late fourteenth century or early fifteenth, depending upon the particular region or sector of the economy concerned, decline set in. By the mid-fifteenth century a severe contraction had occurred in almost every sector of the economy. Why the later fourteenth-century boom came to an end, and why the reversal was of such dramatic proportions, are difficult questions to which only speculative answers can be given. We can be certain that England's economy, and in particular her overseas trade, was gravely injured by wars with France, Spain and the Hanseatic League, and it is possible that a progressive shortage of money may have assisted in the promotion of recession. A further possibility is that the continuing fall in the population, and the consequent increasingly acute shortage of labour may eventually have undermined the buoyancy of the economy, and may have encouraged a shift towards a relatively prosperous self-sufficiency. But if doubts exist about the causes they do not exist about the consequences. On the vast majority of the rural estates that have been studied aggregate rents, rents per acre, and the amount of land under cultivation declined, to reach a nadir around the mid-century or somewhat later. One by one, with very few exceptions, the older and larger urban centres eventually succumbed to economic and demographic retrenchment as the fifteenth century wore on. Exports of wool and cloth, expressed in terms of value, followed a fluctuating but nevertheless distinctly downward course, with a reduction of almost a third comparing 1381–1400 with 1451–80. The production, and probably also the export, of tin followed a similar but less erratic and even steeper downward course. Poundage receipts from duties levied upon the import and export of miscellaneous goods (which, unsatisfactory though they are, probably give a further clue to commercial and industrial prosperity) reached a nadir in the 1450s and 60s, fully 50 per cent below the opening two decades of the century. Wine imports too were more than 50 per cent lower on average between 1450 and 1470 than they had been between 1400 and 1420 [15: *193*]. Thus, even if full account is taken of the compensation to be found in the development of new industrial centres and of the likelihood of grave inefficiency in the collection of customs and other dues during the civil war period, one is forced to conclude that the first sixty or seventy years of the fifteenth century, in aggregate terms at least, bore far more resemblance to Postan's tale of 'recession, arrested economic development and declining national income' [12: *161*] than to Bridbury's proclamation of an 'astonishing record of resurgent vitality and enterprise' [2: *24*].

When considering the significance of such data for the reconstruction of the history of population, it must be stressed that fluctuations in industrial output and commercial activity can normally provide only the vaguest of hints, while even the assistance given by prices, wages and agrarian evidence is sometimes oblique and very difficult to interpret. Yet these downward shifts in economic activity were so general in scope and so dramatic in scale as to be incompatible with a modestly rising or even a stable population. In the absence of population decline the contraction in economic activity must have been accompanied by comparably dramatic reductions in output per head, and by reductions in income to match. In the light of the considerable evidence we have of the well-being of the mass of fifteenth-century Englishmen such a proposition is wholly untenable.

(a) *Agriculture and the Land*

Since the great bulk of Englishmen gained their livelihood by working the land it is essential that we pay careful attention to the testimony, drawn from most parts of the country, of a severely depressed land market, including retreating cultivation, low and falling rents, and wide gaps between the profits that landlords claimed and the incomes that they actually received. For most estates and regions the descent from the post-Black Death peaks of demand for land was under way before 1400, precipitated by, or coinciding with a sharp fall in the price of agricultural commodities and a further rise in wage-rates. Once begun the

36

downward trend usually continued with only occasional respite until the bottom of the trough was reached in the middle of the fifteenth century or a little later. There were notable exceptions but this general pattern appears to have been followed in the great majority of the regions of the country that have so far been studied, while even the exceptional regions experienced a sympathetic mid-century recession.

Before we embark on our brief tour of rural England it should be noted that the authors of the estate and regional studies which are our guides had differing interests and therefore concentrated upon different aspects of agrarian history; some, for example, have dwelt upon landlords' incomes to the neglect of the amount of land under cultivation or the level of rents per acre, while the prime interests of others have lain in social rather than economic matters. Nevertheless we can make some use of most studies.

Northern England is no longer a closed book. The fortunes of the Percy family are well enough known: despite the sparseness of manorial documentation it appears that its income between 1416 and 1470 from lands in Cumberland fell by between quarter and a third, and from lands in Northumberland by up to a half, while that from lands in Yorkshire fell by between a fifth and a quarter after 1443 [55: 12–42]. Still in the far north, we learn that Durham Priory found it extremely difficult, and on occasion impossible, to lease manors in the late 1430s and the 1440s, even at substantially reduced rents [64: ch. 8], while the landed revenues of the bishops of Durham appear to have suffered to an even greater extent [64: 283n.; 95: 69–70]. Conditions in the north-west were scarcely more prosperous, for the agrarian economy of the West Riding, as exemplified by the estates of Bolton Priory, experienced a severe mid-fifteenth-century depression with a marked contraction of arable farming [81: 180–3]. Cheshire and north Shropshire, if we may judge from the estates of the Earls of Shrewsbury and Princes of Wales, after some buoyant decades in the later fourteenth century, displayed abundant evidence of progressive agrarian contraction in the course of the first half of the fifteenth [87]. It has been estimated that the terms on which farms on the Duchy of Lancaster estates were let, already declining by 1400, fell a further 20 per cent in the first seventy-five years of the fifteenth century [13: 237]. That portion of the vast inheritance situated in Staffordshire and Derbyshire appears to bear out this figure, and although some initial resistance to decline was offered in upland pastoral regions, these eventually followed the path trodden by lowland manors since Henry IV's reign and likewise experienced falling rents and abandoned holdings [57: 94 ff.; 58: 84; see also 94: 216–17, 248–50, 265–6].

The fifteenth century was a period of acute agricultural recession in the Midlands. Inadequate documentation is a problem for Leicestershire, but we can be certain that a fall of only 15 per cent in the customary rents due to Leicester Abbey between the rental of 1408 and that of 1477 masks a far more serious state of affairs in which revenues from wool sales, sales of tithe corn, and demesne leases may well have fallen by a half or more [77: 85–8]. The decline in demand for land on the Worcestershire, Gloucestershire and Warwickshire estates of the bishopric of Worcester was so severe that by the 1430s tenants were able to withhold the payment of rent on a grand scale, with the result that arrears mounted relentlessly [68]. Complementary evidence from south Warwickshire and Herefordshire suggests that the bishops' problems were shared by other landlords [6: 161–73; 90: 173–5], while an apparent decline of nearly 50 per cent in the agricultural profits of the Earls of Stafford from their Gloucestershire estates suggests that bad management also played a part [16: 597]. We also learn that on Westminster Abbey manors in Gloucestershire and Worcestershire 'such demesne rents as were not stationary in the first half of the fifteenth century were falling' [74: 23]. Moving eastwards, we find a severe agricultural depression in south Lincolnshire, occasioned by an inability to find tenants for many holdings [72], while Ramsey Abbey, with estates situated mainly in Huntingdonshire and west Cambridgeshire, was experiencing 'the deepest and most prolonged depression in manorial revenues . . . revealed for any period in the abbey history', and by the 1450s and 1460s the accumulation of debt 'was often phenomenal' [88: 265–6, 292–3]. Crowland Abbey, whose estates were largely in Lincolnshire, Huntingdonshire and Northamptonshire, was in a state of 'economic confusion' in the fifteenth century and was suffering in particular from a continual loss of tenants [85: 145–55].

Although it may well prove to be the case that southern counties did not experience as deep as agricultural recession as the rest of England, there are many indications that here too demand for land generally declined significantly in the course of the first half of the fifteenth century. The Berkshire manors studied by R. J. Faith displayed symptoms of falling demand for land occasioned by falling population [69], while in Sussex evidence of decline may be drawn from the estates of Battle Abbey [91: 368–9], the Percies [55: 17–21], and elsewhere [94: 217; 59: 69–72; 60]. The agricultural profits of the bishopric of Winchester, derived predominantly from manors in Hampshire, undoubtedly suffered to some extent, and the 'comparative resilience' that they displayed may well have owed much to the avaricious energies of Cardinal Beaufort [16: 597]; most other landlords in Hampshire seem to have fared less well [98: 421–3]. The recession in Wiltshire and Somerset, as elsewhere, appears to have affected arable farming to a somewhat greater extent than pastoral. Nevertheless the rent roll of the Wiltshire manors of the Duchy of Lancaster generally decreased between c.1400 and c.1470, with receipts from some manors falling by 25–30 per cent, and we learn that leases on the Somerset and Wiltshire manors of Glastonbury Abbey fell by about a third over the same period, with an even greater decline registered in the level of entry fines exacted from customary tenants [86: ch. 9; 99: 40–2; 13: 237].

The evidence briefly recited above clearly suggests that England experienced a deep and widespread agricultural recession in the fifteenth century, a recession which took the form of falling demand for land and falling aggregate production. Yet it would be unrealistic to expect that fifteenth-century England did not have its exceptional regions and exceptional landlords, or that the agricultural recession plunged landlords from affluence to penury. It was inevitable, given the diversity and complexity of the English economy, that demand for land should have been sustained or even enhanced in some regions, and that some landlords, by a combination of diligence, cupidity and good fortune, should have managed to stabilise or even increase their revenues. But, whereas it is essential that full weight must be given to each example of 'prosperity' that comes to light, it would be quite erroneous to attempt to create a new orthodoxy from the unorthodox, or to imagine that untypical upward movements in rents or landlords' revenues were invariably the result of upward movements in the level of population. In a recent attempt to argue that the fifteenth century was not a landlord's purgatory, it has been tentatively suggested that declining incomes were more a sign of incompetent management than of adverse economic circumstances, and that efficiently administered estates, such as those belonging to Christ Church, Canterbury, the Archbishop of Canterbury, Tavistock Abbey, and the Greys of Ruthin, were capable of producing stable or even increasing profits [9: *ch*. 2]. But a close examination of these and other 'prosperous' estates reveals a number of instances in which the degree of 'prosperity' has been exaggerated or based upon inadequate evidence, but no indication of general demographic vitality.

Kent is frequently cited, along with other Home Counties, as a region which escaped the general agrarian depression of the fifteenth century. Kentish agriculture undoubtedly benefited from close proximity to London, for London continued to grow rapidly in the later Middle Ages. Whereas the capital accounted for 2 per cent of the assessed wealth of the country in 1334, by 1515 it accounted for nearly 9 per cent [19]. Yet the most that can be said for Kentish agriculture is that the decline in its fortunes was not as severe as that experienced by most other counties, and that its recovery was stronger and began earlier – in other words its experience differed by degree rather than by kind.

We should not be misled into believing that the rebuilding at immense cost of the nave and the great tower of Canterbury Cathedral was the product of a rising income enjoyed by Christ Church Priory. Indeed, contrary to what has been claimed, far from being immune to the common afflictions of fifteenth-century landlords, the priory suffered the common fate of declining income. The record gross revenues of £4100 in 1411 should be seen in the context of only £2382 received in 1437, £2116 in 1454 and £2060 in 1456 – this much can be learnt from Smith's study which touched only lightly on the fifteenth century [93: *13*]. Conclusive evidence of decline is provided in a recent study of the late medieval fortunes of the priory in which we are told that the gross manorial charge, taking no account of arrears, fell by 22 per cent between 1410 and 1469, and that, although many examples of temporary recoveries in rent levels occurred during this period, the over-all trend was unmistakably downwards. Furthermore, we learn not only that rents were depressed in the middle decades of the century, but also that the priory's income suffered acutely at this time from the accumulation of arrears [62: *95–125*].

Such evidence, firmly based upon the direct testimony of manorial accounts, suggests that the picture that has emerged from

F. R. H. Du Boulay's study of the comparatively poorly documented estates of the archbishopric, situated predominantly in the same region, may well be too optimistic. In the absence of an adequate range of reeves' and receivers' accounts Du Boulay was forced to rely primarily upon valors for evidence of long-term fluctuations in the archbishopric's income [65]. In fact only four valors survive for a period of two and a half centuries, namely for 1291, 1422, 1446 and 1535. Thus evidence of the extent of the decline, if any, in income in the decades preceding 1422 and succeeding 1446, is completely lacking, a grave weakness since the trough of the decline in the value of Christ Church Priory's lands was not reached until the late 1460s. It has often been noted that valors can be a notoriously treacherous source: in particular they are statements of potential income and not of the revenues which were collected or even ultimately collectable.[13] It is significant therefore to find that according to the best of the surviving series of receivers' accounts the average annual amount actually received by the archbishops' officials from the bailiwick of Otford, which according to the valors should have been worth £346 in 1422 and £413 in 1446, was no more than £303 in the 1450s, £262 in the 1460s, and £308 in the 1470s.[14] Clearly we should pay close attention to Du Boulay's judgement that the estate passed through 'a phase of mid-century doldrums . . . when it became rather harder to make satisfactory leases' [66: 220, 225].

Similar doubts can be expressed about some of the claims concerning the basis of the prosperity of the Greys of Ruthin, whose lands lay for the most part in the east Midlands [80]. While it is evident that this noble family benefited greatly from the longevity of heads of the house, a rare absence of minorities, prudent management, and skilful avoidance of the major pitfalls of war and politics, there is insufficient evidence for us to be certain that income from the individual manors which compromised its landed estates did not decline in the course of the fifteenth century. Inevitably the small cluster of extant sources, comprising in the main a single valor dated 1467–8 and two receivers' accounts from the mid-1440s, reveals little about agrarian trends in the first half of the century, but it should be noted that the amounts entered under 'decays of rent' in 1467–8 indicate that a decline of 15 per cent had taken place in this source of income since the last rental had been composed. Furthermore, although comparison with an extent made in 1392, of certain of the manors while they were in the hands of the Hastings family, suggests that their yield had not fallen by 1468, we are warned that the 'Hastings estate was in some disrepair by 1392', and that the value of these manors 'may therefore have been lower than usual' [80:28–9]. Thus the fortunes of the fifteenth-century Greys cannot be held to have depended upon a rising demand for their lands, still less upon the recovery of population. Similarly, the Hungerfords' rapid social and economic advance appears to have owed far more to good political judgement and high salaries from the holding of office in royal bureaucracies, than to profits forthcoming from their extensive Wiltshire rent-rolls and sheep farms. For the Hungerfords, as well as the Percies, the key to wealth lay in the accumulation of more lands rather than the extraction of greater profits from existing lands [82; 86].

The land market of the south-west displayed exceptional resilience in the later Middle Ages, yet even here there were some severely depressed areas. The prosperity of east and central Cornwall and east Devon, where rents rose to new heights in the fifteenth century and scarcely any vacant holdings were to be found, must be balanced against the more conventional fortunes of west Cornwall and south Devon, where rents fell and vacant holdings abounded. Moreover the economy of the whole region experienced a significant downturn in the middle decades of the fifteenth century. Although it would be unwise to discount completely the possibility of a less than average decrease in the population of the south-west, the buoyancy of the local economy would seem to have played the major part in the maintenance of land values. The increasing rent rolls enjoyed by landlords fortunate to have estates in the prosperous parts of the south-west were less the result of land-hunger than of a selective demand for favourably sited fertile soils; the rents of poor and ill-sited soils stagnated or declined. The contrasts between the fortunes of different parts of the region were heightened by high levels of mobility among the population. For these reasons it would be unwise to argue for general demographic vitality from the fortunes of the south-west [70; 71; 76; 78].

After our examination of the English economy in the second half of the fourteenth century it is scarcely necessary to warn against any simple correlation between the level of population and the level of economic activity, even in the agrarian sector. In addition our knowledge of the agrarian sector is perforce composed of the experience of a series of individual estates, and there were many factors, other than the numbers of people, which could affect the receipts, rent levels and occupation of holdings on a single estate. For example, the landlord who adopted flexible and imaginative policies to cope with changed economic circumstances might compete successfully for tenants with his more conservative peers. It must also be stressed that the land market was constrained by custom, and that for a time some landlords successfully used their seigneurial authority to force tenants to remain on their holdings and pay, in both money and labour, rents in excess of the true market value of the land. On the other hand it is essential that we should not regard peasants as mere flotsam drifting on the tide of economic fortune and seigneurial authority. On the contrary the peasantry frequently took steps to exploit the power that declining demand for land had given them, including refusal to pay rents or other dues, and the abandonment of holdings on a grand scale if the terms of the tenancies were not acceptable [7]. Some account must also be taken of the adverse effects of border raids and military campaigns on the economies of estates situated in the far north and west, although they do not appear to have been decisive [64: 274–5; 87: 560].

In spite of the difficulties of interpretation, however, the great weight of the agrarian evidence, the scale and uniformity of the changes in the occupation and value of land between the late fourteenth century and the late fifteenth are such as to be virtually incapable of explanation without recourse to population decline. The thesis of fifteenth-century population decline, supported as it is by the direct demographic evidence discussed earlier, is further strengthened by the contention of those who have studied the phenomenon of the deserted village, that the most rapid depopulation of all occurred between 1450 and 1485 [56: 11–17], and by the well-attested conclusion that retreating cultivation took place alongside a dramatic increase in the average size of holdings and a dramatic decrease in the numbers of labouring poor [17: 139 ff.]. Furthermore, firmer and more precise evidence of the course of population is beginning to emerge from the painstakingly detailed study of manorial court rolls, a new and promising avenue of research into medieval society. A by-product of the intimate knowledge which follows from the amassing of minute data on individuals and families is that researchers are able to make informed projections of the probable course of population on the manors they have studied. In the two such studies which have so far been published the authors are in no doubt that the population of their manors declined substantially. E. A. DeWindt tells us that, 'It is definite . . . that Holywell [Hunts.] was experiencing a decline in resident population from as early as the second decade of the fourteenth century and on into the 1450s.' The scale of this decline was prodigious: 64 per cent between 1300 and 1450 [63: *166–71*]. J. A. Raftis has found a somewhat different chronology at Warboys (Hunts.), but a similar trend. A partial recovery in population took place on this manor after the Black Death, but from 1370, 'a steady and prolonged decline set in. This was most drastic after 1400, so that by the mid-fifteenth century the population would seem to have been less than one half of that one hundred and fifty years earlier' [89: *68*].

There would, therefore, appear to be no doubt that there were substantially fewer people in the countryside in the mid-fifteenth century than there had been fifty or sixty years before. If one is not inclined to accept that the population of England declined during this period, the only possible alternative explanation must lie in a truly prodigious expansion of the non-agrarian sectors of the economy which gave employment to those who were clearly no longer on the land. It is not a difficult task to demonstrate that such an explanation has no substance whatsoever.

(b) *Towns, Trade and Industry*

In order for the urban, industrial and commercial sectors of the economy to have offered any compensation for decline in the rural population the numbers absorbed by them would have had to grow not only relatively but absolutely. In order for these sectors to have offered complete compensation they would have had to grow at a rate approximately nine times greater than the rate at which numbers in the agricultural sector were falling. Thus, for the sake of argument, in order to compensate for a fall of only 10 per cent in the agricultural population the numbers living in towns and employed in industry and trade would have had to almost double. While it is possible that the non-agricultural sectors continued in the fifteenth century to grow relative to the agricultural, and just possible, although most unlikely, that they grew a little in absolute terms, growth on any greater scale simply cannot be contemplated. We have already noted the sharp decline recorded in the first half of the fifteenth century in those branches of industry and overseas trade for which data exist, and even the most optimistic commentator on the fortunes of the late medieval urban sector readily admits that, 'most provincial towns had many fewer inhabitants after the Black Death than before it' [2: 62]. Those who take a more pessimistic view would see the period from c.1420 to c.1550 as one of relentless urban economic decline and demographic attrition [111].

With towns as with agriculture, however, the more closely one looks at the evidence the more one appreciates that generalisations are hazardous. Not only does account have to be taken of the varying fortunes of the older towns, large and small, but also of the many industrial villages which grew into sizeable settlements in this period. Looking first at the older centres, there can be little doubt that there was a substantial overall decline in both their populations and their prosperity. Of the dozen or more leading towns of late fourteenth-century England, all with populations of 4000 or more, fewer than half, most notably London, Colchester, Salisbury and Newcastle, appear to have successfully resisted substantial decline as the fifteenth century wore on. Of the forty or so towns with populations in 1377 of between 1000 and 4000 those which resisted decline or advanced to new peaks of population and posperity – for example Exeter, Plymouth, Worcester, Reading and Ipswich – were far outnumbered by those which succumbed. This is not to say that a great many of these older towns did not continue to enjoy a fair measure of trade, rather that in terms of both total population and aggregate economic activity there were few which did not contract between the later fourteenth century and the close of the fifteenth.[15]

There are clear signs that changes in the distribution of wealth and in consumption patterns profoundly affected the structure of the late medieval economy; in particular they led to shifts in the location of industries, and to changes in the nature of the industries themselves and the articles which they produced. We must not be over-impressed, therefore, with evidence of contraction in the older urban centres, for this contraction was undoubtedly compensated to an appreciable extent by growth in newer centres and in rural industries. Just as the expanding cloth industry, based primarily upon the production of cloth suitable for the mass market, provided the foundation of the prosperity of most of the older towns which resisted the general decline, so it also encouraged the spectacular development of many villages into thriving towns. Notable examples of such development in the south-west include Totnes and Tiverton; in Suffolk and north Essex, Hadleigh, Maldon, Lavenham, Nayland, Long Melford, Sudbury and Coggeshall; in the West Riding, Leeds, Bradford, Halifax and Wakefield; and in the Cotswolds, Castle Combe, Stroudwater (& district) [2: *112–13*; 102; 108; 110]. Some of the metal trades also enjoyed substantial growth. The manufacture of pewter, to satisfy the fashionable desires of the gentry, bourgeoisie and richer peasant alike, was one of the few exclusively urban industries to expand rapidly [107: *ch. 2*], while the primarily rural iron-working industries of north Worcestershire and south Staffordshire stimulated the development of Birmingham and its environs [6: *86–7*].

In light of the evidence of variations in agrarian and industrial prosperity recited above it should come as no surprise to learn that profound changes took place in the regional distribution of population and wealth in later medieval England. A comparison of the distribution of taxable wealth between counties in 1334 and 1515 reveals that the position of counties south of a line from the Severn estuary to the Wash improved markedly *vis-à-vis* that of counties to the north [19]. The most impressive performances were recorded by Cornwall, Devon, Somerset, a group of counties surrounding London, namely Middlesex, Surrey, Kent and Hertfordshire, and the clothworking counties of Essex and Suffolk. We know that peasant families were surprisingly mobile [7: *32–5*; 84], and a comparative study of the 1377 Poll Tax returns and Tudor subsidy and muster returns will doubtless reveal that a major redistribution of population accompanied this redistribution of wealth. More detailed investigation will also reveal that major redistributions of population and wealth took place within as well as between counties.

Thus in the England of the fifteenth century, as in the Britain of the 1920s and 30s, the depression was punctuated by instances of striking growth and development. These instances helped to balance the decline taking place in other centres of industry and trade, but even the cloth industry did not grow at a rate sufficient to have offered significant compensation for the overall decline in the rural population. We have learnt that the major concentrations of clothworkers provided a strong stimulus to the economies of their hinterlands, but in national terms the impact was much more limited. It has been estimated, on the basis of stable home demand, that the cloth industry employed 23–26,000 more people at the end of the fourteenth century than at the beginning [101: *261 n.*]; but even allowing for further increases thereafter it is probable that at the very most an additional 2 per cent of the population found some employment in clothworking. Much of this employment was, moreover, of a part-time character, consisting of the labour of peasant families who continued to devote most of their time to farming.

Since our primary concern is the reconstruction of the course of the national population we have dwelt upon absolute size and absolute levels of production and employment, and have freely used such words as 'depression', 'recession', 'decline' and 'contraction'. But we should not forget that the most valid measure of economic prosperity results from dividing the total numbers of people into such aggregates. The 'depression' of the fifteenth century was no ordinary depression since it did not involve falling *per capita* output, falling living standards or rising unemployment. A careful distinction needs to be made, therefore, between changes in the total area of land in cultivation, the total size of the urban sector, the total output of industry, the total amount of goods imported and exported, and these changes measured in terms of the size of the prevailing population of England. That the fall in population generally exceeded the fall in production is suggested by the behaviour of real wages.

(iii) WAGES, PRICES AND THE SUPPLY OF MONEY

Much expert attention has been devoted to the interpretation of medieval and early modern wage and price data, and many attempts have been made since Professor Postan's pioneering article in 1950 to utilise them for demographic purposes. Fortunately the accumulation of a wide range of direct and indirect demographic evidence means that it is no longer necessary to attach prime importance to these data, and yet if they are employed with discretion they can still play a useful supporting role. Discretion must be employed, however, since wages and prices are blunt instruments in the hands of the historical demographer, and although they are fully capable of reflecting large-scale shifts in the level of population, they are much less informative in less spectacular periods. The level of population was undoubtedly a major determinant of the level of wages and prices, but other factors may have played a part, including the amount of money in the nation and the speed with which it circulated. The prices of foodstuffs were also influenced by such diverse, and to us frequently obscure, factors as changes in the size of the non-agrarian sectors of the economy, in the balance between pastoral and arable farming, in the levels of exports and imports, and in the weather and the state of technology; while wages were influenced by custom and legislation as well as by the supply of labour and the demand for it. Nor should we neglect, given the experience of our own times, the fact that prices can exert a powerful influence on wages just as wages can exert a powerful influence on prices.

Yet even having regard to all these reservations it cannot be denied that the behaviour of wages between 1350 and 1500 offers strong supporting evidence of substantial long-term population decline. Data from many parts of the country, a small selection of which is printed in Table II, suggest a striking uniformity of change in the course of the last 150 years of the Middle Ages. With occasional reverses both day- and piece-rates for both agricultural and building work climbed upwards to reach a peak somewhere between 1430 and 1460. Sadly the series of agricultural wages are the least satisfactory, but an increase of around 50 to 75 per cent between 1340–9 and 1440–9 in wages paid for threshing and winnowing is indicated, and the true rate may well have been higher.[16] The many good series of building workers' wages record increases over the same century of between 75 and 100 per cent for craftsmen, and 100 and 125 per cent for labourers.[17] Of especial significance is the fact that substantial increases were often recorded in the fifteenth century. This evidence suggests a severe shortage of labour in late medieval England, a suggestion for which there is abundant confirmation in a multitude of non-quantifiable sources, ranging from the frequent reiterations of the Statutes of Labourers to the complaints of individual employers as far apart as the Cornish tin mines and the fertile lowlands of southern Sussex [106: *63–5*; 61: *93, 98*].

Taking the period as a whole, the course of prices generally ran counter to that of wages. But although the century and a half after

Table II

Wage Rates, 1301–1540

| | Piece-rates for threshing and winnowing 3 rased quarters of grains (wheat, barley, oats) | | | Daily wage rates of craftsmen and labourers | | | | | | | |
| | | | | Average of rates on 8 Winchester Manors | | | | Rates paid for building work in Westminster | | | |
	(a) Westminster Manors	(b) Winchester Manors	(c) Thorold Rogers	(d) Carpenter	(e) Thatcher and helper	(f) Labourer	(g) Tiler and helper	(h) Carpenter	(i) Labourer	(j) Mason	(k) Tiler and helper
	d.	d.	d.	d.	d.	d.	d.	d.	d.	d.	d.
1301–10	6·51	3·85		2·82	3·19	1·49	6·19				
1311–20	8·01	4·05		3·41	3·55	1·87	6·44				
1321–30	6·68	4·62		3·39	3·78	1·84	5·91				
1331–40	7·35	4·92		3·18	3·82	1·78	5·73				
1341–50	7·41	5·03		2·96	3·73	1·86	4·70	3·89	2·12	6·13	9·00
1351–60	13·02	5·18		3·92	5·00	2·85	6·25	6·06	3·08	6·52	11·92
1361–70	12·76	6·10	7·20	4·29	5·95	3·25	7·01	7·94	4·27	7·35	10·50
1371–80	12·23	7·00	8·70	4·32	5·98	3·19	6·89	6·00	3·39	7·21	10·00
1381–90	10·82	7·22	9·03	4·40	6·01	3·35	7·54	6·42	3·33	6·48	11·51
1391–1400	10·44	7·23	7·66	4·13	5·85	3·30	7·36	5·68	3·46	6·67	12·50
1401–10	11·00	7·31	8·37	4·64	6·31	3·53	8·17	—	3·33	6·67	11·88
1411–20	12·40	7·35	8·50	4·51	6·40	3·69	8·50	6·22	4·00	6·67	12·99
1421–30	10·00	7·34	8·13	4·52	6·19	3·83	8·56	6·77	3·84	6·67	13·20
1431–40	13·00	7·30	9·75	4·75	6·89	3·87	8·81	7·00	4·87	6·67	13·17
1441–50	13·00	7·33	9·13	5·18	8·19	4·11	9·24	8·17	4·91	6·67	12·74
1451–60	—	7·25	8·75	5·23	8·24	4·03	9·60	7·57	4·64	6·67	13·00
1461–70	—	—	8·50	—	—	—	—	8·00	4·42	6·67	13·00
1471–80	—	—	8·00	—	—	—	—	7·45	4·06	6·67	13·00
1481–90	—	—	7·00	—	—	—	—	6·63	4·03	6·67	12·31
1491–1500	—	—	9·25	—	—	—	—	6·27	4·00	6·67	11·50
1501–10	—	—	11·63	—	—	—	—	6·66	4·07	6·67	12·75
1511–20	—	—	10·00	—	—	—	—	6·64	4·02	6·67	12·24
1521–30	—	—	11·25	—	—	—	—	7·61	4·04	6·67	—
1531–40	—	—	12·25	—	—	—	—	8·00	4·00	6·67	—

SOURCES: Beveridge [118: 28; 117: 38], Thorold Rogers [128: I, 320; IV, 525].

the Black Death has frequently been termed an era of falling agricultural prices a detailed appraisal of the evidence, some of which is contained in Table III, shows that this is only partly true. In fact grain prices in the second quarter of the fourteenth century were the *lowest* they were ever to be, while in the third quarter of the same century they were maintained at levels comparable with the *highest* ever hitherto seen. From the mid-1370s, however, grain prices began to fall sharply and by the 1380s and 90s a decline of 25 to 30 per cent had taken place. The opening decades of the fifteenth century saw a partial recovery before prices turned downwards again in mid-century; by the closing decades a hesitant recovery was under way. During the same period the prices of livestock and dairy produce, although falling, displayed greater resilience than those of grains, probably due in part to changes in tastes brought about by the improved living standards of the masses [128; *i, 452, iv, 381;* 115:*163;* 15:*209*]. For an over-all view we cannot at present do better than study the behaviour of the price of the Phelps Brown/Hopkins 'composite unit of consumables', composed 80 per cent of foodstuffs and drink and 20 per cent of textiles and fuel, which fell sharply in the later 1370s, recovered somewhat in the first quarter of the fifteenth century, and then plunged to new post-Black Death lows between 1440 and 1479 [125].

The effects of these divergent price and wage movements upon the real wage-rates of common people were dramatic. Staying with the researches of Professor Phelps Brown and Sheila Hopkins we learn that the real wage-rates of Oxford building craftsmen, taking the 1340s as a base, had risen by almost 50 per cent by the last quarter of the fourteenth century and almost 100 per cent by the later fifteenth century, at which time they were higher than they were ever to be again before the later nineteenth century (see Figure 2, p. 71). Naturally these precise figures cannot be applied to the whole community. Indeed since England was primarily a peasant economy wages comprised only a fraction of the real income of the population as a whole; nevertheless they do provide further indications of a general rise in living standards. To use the language of the economist, the real wage was a measure of the marginal productivity of labour, and this in turn must have been closely related to the welfare of the population at large.

Argument about the precise weighting to be given to the various factors which may have played a part in causing these movements in wages and prices is certain to continue, but it is most unlikely that falling population, which reduced the supply of labour relative to that of capital and land, was not of prime importance in the fifteenth century as well as the later fourteenth.

Table III
Wheat Prices, 1301–1540

Decennial Means in shillings per quarter

	Exeter		Westminster		'Eng. average'	
	s.	Index (1341–50) =100	s.	Index (1341–9) =100	s.	Index (1341–50) =100
1301–10					5·7	119
1311–20	8·4	168			7·9	164
1321–30	6·4	128			6·8	142
1331–40	5·4	108			5·2	108
1341–50	5·0	100	4·3	100	4·8	100
1351–60	7·1	122	7·2	167	7·0	146
1361–70	8·3	166	9·0	209	8·0	167
1371–80	6·8	136	6·8	158	6·7	140
1381–90	5·5	110	5·0	116	5·2	108
1391–1400	5·1	102	5·4	126	5·5	115
1401–10	6·5	130	7·7	179	6·4	133
1411–20	6·3	126	6·9	161	5·8	121
1421–30	5·7	114	6·1	142	5·5	115
1431–40	7·3	146	8·8	205	7·3	152
1441–50	5·4	108	6·1	142	4·9	102
1451–60	6·4	128	6·9	160		
1461–70	6·3	126	6·3	147		
1471–80	6·2	124	7·8	181		
1481–90	6·9	138	7·6	177		
1491–1500	6·0	120	6·1	142		
1501–10	7·3	146	7·3	170		
1511–20	6·8	136	7·6	177		
1521–30	8·6	172	8·4	195		
1531–40	8·4	168	7·8	181		

SOURCES: Beveridge [116; 117:*38*; 118:*28*]. The dating used by Beveridge has been altered to conform with the usual practice of dating an account by its closing Michaelmas.

Half of the rise in real wage-rates recorded by the Phelps Brown/Hopkins index occurred after 1400, and as we have seen from our glance at the fortunes of towns, industry and commerce, they could not have been forced up to these levels by a rising demand for labour in these sectors. On the contrary, the rising wages of the first seventy-five years of the fifteenth century must be interpreted in the context of substantially declining economic activity and the presence of strong deflationary pressures in the economy. In like fashion the behaviour of agricultural prices fits well into a context of falling population. In particular we should note that food became cheaper in a period when the acreage under cultivation shrank and *per capita* consumption probably increased substantially. By the mid-fifteenth century annual fluctuations in price caused by variations in the quality of the harvest were among the narrowest in recorded history. That this abundance was not assisted by grain imports is clear from both statutes and customs accounts. Between 1394 and 1467 successive Acts of Parliament shifted national policy decisively from the complete prohibition of grain exports to free exports and a prohibition on imports, save only in times of exceptional scarcity. That this shift in policy was occasioned by economic rather than political considerations is exemplified by the many petitions to Parliament which complain, as in 1437, that 'farmers could not sell their corn at a profitable rate', and as in 1445, that 'the counties on the sea could not sell the bulk of their corn other than by oversea traffic'. The growing export trade in grain is a further indication of abundance [105: *131–56*].

On *a priori* grounds alone, however, it would be unwise to place the explanation for price movements solely on population and other 'real' factors; prices may be influenced by the quantity of money in circulation as well as by shifts in supply and demand. Indeed a number of historians have argued that a shortage of money was the prime factor behind the falling prices of the later Middle Ages, and some have gone so far as to suggest that the shortage of money exerted so powerful a depressive influence over the whole economy that it was instrumental in causing the falling production and trade of the fifteenth century [123; 127; 129]. In support of their arguments we find that the annual average output of coin from English mints plunged dramatically after the mid-fourteenth century and fell by a further 50 per cent comparing 1350–1417 with 1418–60, and that frequent complaints were made about the shortage of specie by groups of merchants and tradesmen [121: *410–14*; 123: *474–7*]. Moreover one notes that the periods of lowest mintings, 1375–1407 and 1438–60, were also periods of low prices.[18]

It is possible therefore that the supply of money may have exercised some influence over price levels, and that its contraction may have contributed in some measure to the economic recession of the fifteenth century. But it is scarcely credible that money supply was a more important influence than population decline on the level of prices and economic activity in late medieval England, and inconceivable that it could be decisive, as some argue, in the face of a recovery of population [123: 479; 129: 71–2]. It is far from proven that the contraction in the total stock of money was by itself sufficiently great to have forced prices down. The output of the mints is a very poor guide to the total stock of money, even in the long term. If, as is frequently maintained, England had a balance-of-payments surplus in the later Middle Ages, foreign coin would have been drawn into the country and augmented the native money supply. It is also probable that credit was used more extensively as time went by, and that this helped to compensate for a fall in the total stock of coins [119; 126], and it is possible that a fall in the total stock of money may have been offset to some extent by an increase in the velocity of circulation of remaining coins. Another major criticism of those who would seek to negate the importance of real factors is that as far as prices are concerned it is not the total stock of money in the country which is the crucial measure, rather it is the stock of money per unit of output and to a lesser extent the stock of money per head [122: 91–2]. From what we know of the output of most goods in the fifteenth century, and of the probable course of population, we can be certain that the decline in the stock of money per unit of output and per head was far less than the decline in the total stock. This may well explain why signs of really acute monetary shortage, for example the widespread adoption of barter, do not appear to be present in fifteenth-century England.

In this century the English currency displayed a remarkable degree of stability, in marked contrast with Continental currencies [119: 419–21]. It is improbable that it could have done so in the face of dire monetary scarcity, since immense pressures would have built up in favour of debasement. Moreover, despite claims to the contrary, there does not appear to have been an acute shortage of bullion in fifteenth-century England. On the contrary visitors to these shores frequently commented upon the huge quantities of silver and gold plate held in both private and institutional hands, and confirmation of these comments can be found in wills and inventories [137: 28–9, 42–3, 77–8; 107: 50–1, 60–1]. If it was felt necessary the Crown could have induced the owners of plate to sell to the mint on favourable terms, thereby greatly increasing the amount of coin in circulation. But the most telling argument of all against relying solely upon monetary explanations is the behaviour of wages, which continued to push upwards during the middle decades of the fifteenth century, commonly believed to be the period of greatest monetary dearth. We can conclude, therefore, that if a shortage of money was exercising a deflationary pressure on the fifteenth-century economy, the behaviour of wages is truly remarkable since it testifies to a growing shortage of labour in conditions normally liable to have produced unemployment. The only satisfactory explanation would seem to lie in a continuing decrease in the size of the population.

4 Why was the Population Decline so Protracted?

ECONOMIC conditions in the fifteenth century were without doubt conducive to an expansion of population: land and food were cheap and abundant, while labour was scarce and well-rewarded. Conditions such as these, according to a multitude of demographers and historians from Malthus at the close of the eighteenth century to the flourishing French school of our own times, should have led to a rising birth-rate and a falling death-rate. The age of marriage should have fallen in response to the availability of land and work, marriages should have become more fertile in response both to improved standards of nutrition and to a lessening of the burdens of parenthood, and the infrequency of subsistence crises should have led to a lowering of the mortality schedules of infants, adolescents and adults alike.[19] In the words of Malthus in the 1790s: 'Plenty of rich land to be had for little or nothing is so powerful a cause of population as generally to overcome all obstacles' [36: *1, 304*], and of Goubert in the 1950s: 'The price of wheat almost always constitutes a true demographic barometer' [28: *468*]. If population had expanded apace in the fifteenth century historians would certainly have had few difficulties in explaining why! Yet, as we have seen, it is manifest that such expansion did not take place. In the light of the evidence at present available to us there would appear to be an overwhelming case for assuming that the level of mortality was the prime determinant of the size of the population, and also for assuming in turn that the level of mortality was not primarily determined by economic factors.

The size of a population is, however, a function of its fertility schedule as well as its mortality schedule, and the severe epidemics of the period sent violent tremors through the social and economic fabric which may well have led to profound changes in attitudes to many aspects of life including marriage and procreation. Accordingly, some historians would seek to explain the failure of numbers to recover by the widespread practising of prudential checks. Professors Helleiner and Duby have tentatively suggested that the improved living conditions of the masses 'so far from promoting early marriages and high marital fertility, may have produced the opposite effects' – namely that, eager to defend their new-found prosperity, peasants and artisans delayed marriage and deliberately limited the size of their families, and that young men increasingly married older women [30: *69–71*; 67: *309–10*]. It will be noted that these arguments have some similarity to those put forward by E. A. Wrigley with reference to later seventeenth-century Colyton [44]. Infanticide practised upon female babies is also mentioned as a possibility. Sylvia Thrupp has tentatively suggested that some people may have sought to evade family responsibilities by entering the Church or leading itinerant lives [40: *118*]. But the lack of sufficient evidence to prove or disprove such hypotheses is highlighted by the fact that Duby espouses precisely the opposite view and argues not only for a 'reduction in the relative numbers of landless labourers', but also that 'peasants settled on their land were probably more careful to limit their families' than were those who led itinerant lives [67: *309–10*].

A fundamental criticism of hypotheses which stress delayed marriages and family limitation is that they would appear to turn logic on its head, by requiring prudential checks to be applied in an era when wives and children could be supported, and indeed owing to the acute shortage of labour could often be self-supporting, and abandoned and not re-applied in the subsequent era of drastically declining living standards from *c*.1520 onwards. Moreover, such evidence as there is seems also directly against them. One of the immediate effects of plague in the fourteenth century – as Hume, Sussmilch and Malthus noted with the epidemics of the eighteenth century – appears to have been an upsurge in the number of marriages.[20] J. Hajnal's analysis of the Poll Tax returns of 1377 suggests that the prevailing marriage rate was high, and that it conformed to the normal 'non-European' pattern [27: *116–20*]. As for the view that young men may increasingly have married older women, we can only reflect that Titow has argued, with more conviction and a stronger foundation of evidence, that land *scarcity* in the thirteenth century frequently drove young men to marry widows [96]. Indeed it seems more logical to believe that the population fell despite an increase in the marriage rate and fertility than to believe that it fell, or failed to recover, because of a decrease in the marriage rate and fertility. But it must be admitted that there are scarcely any reliable data on these basic aspects of medieval life, and that there is a pressing need for more research.

Postan would see the level of population both influencing and being influenced by 'upward and downward trends in medieval agriculture'. He entertains the possibility that population, which in his view began to fall before the Black Death and may have continued to fall after the power of plague had waned, was influenced by a long-term agrarian crisis and decline in the productivity of the soil. In Postan's own words, 'the continual inability of men to repair the damage done to the land in previous centuries may have been one of the causes of delayed recovery' [17:38–9; see also 14:233–6; 16:569–70]. So it may, but before one could allow soil exhaustion a leading role the case would have to be made in greater detail, and low productivity of the soil would have to be reconciled with low prices for agricultural produce and a striking freedom from subsistence crises.

Having placed the emphasis upon high mortality caused by disease we must now explore the mechanisms through which it could have operated upon late medieval society. At the outset it must be stressed that it is mistaken to assume that demographic decline could only be effected by national epidemics of spectacular proportions. On the contrary there is every reason to believe that the cumulative impact of lesser and local epidemics could be decisive, the more so if the young were afflicted in disproportionately high numbers. From the last quarter of the fourteenth century plague increasingly occurred in the form of innumerable widely scattered local outbreaks. Notwithstanding, in little more than a century after 1377 England experienced at least fifteen outbreaks of plague and/or other epidemic diseases of national or extra-regional proportions; namely, 1379–83, 1389–93, 1400, 1405–7, 1413, 1420, 1427, 1433–4, 1438–9, 1457–8, 1463–4, 1467, 1471, 1479–80 and 1485. As most of these outbreaks have received detailed attention in other works it is necessary to comment only upon those that have not. Although not noted by chroniclers as a national outbreak, there is considerable evidence that 1420 saw severe epidemics in many parts of the realm, including Norfolk, Kent, London, Scotland and the north of England [33: 316; 47: 221–2; 53:143, 150]. In 1427 the cause of the high mortality was not plague but 'a certain rheumy infirmity called *mure* [which] invaded the whole people, and so infected the aged along with the younger that it conducted a great number into the grave' [47: *398*]. In the closing years of the 1450s, we learn, a 'great and grievous plague' afflicted Kent and many other parts of England [139: *67*].

Much more attention must be paid than hitherto to diseases other than plague, for there can be no doubt that they played a major part in raising the death-rate in the fifteenth century, as they did in all centuries of pre-industrial England. The outbreak of 1427 was only one of many fatal pulmonary epidemics in the 1420s; and we know that between 1389 and 1393 famine-sickness and dysentery were rife; that many deaths were precipitated in 1438–9 by the one major famine of the century; and that in 1485 the cause of the high mortality was the 'sweat'. As yet we know little of the precise incidence of diseases such as typhus, diphtheria, measles, dysentery and the various pox and fevers, and scarcely anything about such mysterious afflictions as 'styche' and 'ipydyme'; nor should tuberculosis, appropriately called the 'Great White Plague', a mass killer in all eras, be ignored. Small wonder that William Langland portrayed the late fourteenth century as an age of

> fevres and fluxes,
> Coughes, and cardiacles, crampes and tothaches
> Rewmes and radegoundes and roynouse scalles,
> Byles, and bocches and brennyng agues;
> Frenesyes, and foule yveles . . .
> . . . pokkes and pestilences'
> (*Piers Plowman*, B Text, Passus xx, 80–4, 97)

Also worthy of special attention is the vexed question of whether bubonic plague exhibits a preference for the younger age-groups. Contemporaries were in no doubt whatsoever that in many of the major epidemics victims were not only selected mainly from the young but also from the male sex. Commentator after commentator from many parts of Europe remarked on the disproportionately large numbers of children and adolescent males who died in the 1360–2 outbreak: the anonymous chronicler of York reports that it was known as '*la mortalite des enfauntz*'; Knighton wrote that the 'great and less died, but especially young men and children', the northern Chronicle of Melsa termed it '*secunda pestilentia* . . .

que dicta est puerorum'; and a London chronicler recorded that 'especially it raged among Young Men and Children, being less fatal to Women'. Moreover, *The Brut*, the *Polychronicon* and John of Reading all remarked that men died in far greater numbers than women. De Chauliac, who was among the most reliable of contemporary reporters on medical matters, relates that in France 'a multitude of boys, and a few women were attacked', a view confirmed from as far afield as Poland [47: *203, 206*; 53: *127–9, 136–8*; 50: *180*; 30: *11*].

The markedly different characteristics ascribed by chroniclers to some later outbreaks clearly demonstrate that it is wrong to dismiss their testimony concerning the age-selective impact of epidemics, as has recently been done, on the grounds that they were misled because 'children were so much in evidence as a result of the birth- and death-rate changes brought about by the first plague' [46: *591 n.*]. The epidemic of 1369 was termed by more than one observer as a pestilence 'of men and the larger animals' [141: *i, 309*], and while certain outbreaks of the later 1370s and the early 1380s were seen to rage 'chiefly among children' [138: *ix, 14, 21*], others were seen as killing 'both men and women without number', 'an infinity of both sexes', and 'sparing no age or sex' [141: *i, 319*; 47: *219*].[21] The 1390–1 pestilence, which was so prolonged and so severe as to warrant comparison with the Black Death itself, naturally attracted much detailed comment from contemporaries. Walsingham called it 'a great plague, especially of youths and young children who died everywhere in towns and villages in incredible and excessive numbers' [141: *ii, 186*], while the anonymous continuator of Ranulph Higden confirmed that it killed more young than old [138: *ix, 237–8*]. Adam of Usk reporting on the epidemic of 1400 described it as a plague which 'prevailed through all England and specially among the young, swift in its attack and carrying off many souls' [131: *207*].

Modern medical opinion, however, is by no means as certain as late medieval chroniclers that plague frequently strikes hardest at the young and the male sex; in fact many specialists maintain that no group is inherently more vulnerable [51: *209*; 53: *138*]. None the less, R. Pollitzer does admit that differences in death-rate might follow from differences in risks of exposure [52: *503–4*]; children were perhaps more likely to come into contact with rats and fleas because they played on floors and in streets among dirt and rubbish. It must be admitted, however, that plague is not only an extremely complex disease, but our medical knowledge of its nature and behaviour is also unsatisfactory because it has been gathered largely from the study of a handful of small outbreaks in this century. The whole subject is further complicated by the strong possibility that there were many strains of *Pasteurella pestis*. Additional explanations of the susceptibility of the young may lie in the fact that those who recover from an attack of plague usually acquire immunity to infection thereafter [49:440], and in the possibility that those who live through an outbreak without becoming infected may, through natural resistance, be less likely to become infected in subsequent outbreaks. Death-rates would therefore tend to be higher among those who had not previously been exposed to infection.

Whereas it is possible, albeit probably misguided, to dismiss the chroniclers as ill-informed and the tale of the Pied Piper of Hamelin as unsubstantiated legend, hard statistics culled from London burial registers present a much more formidable obstacle to the sceptical. Such statistics, from the parish of St Botolph's Without Bishopsgate during the 1603 plague outbreak, have recently been published by M. F. and T. H. Hollingsworth [31]. Using registers which record age at death as well as allowing sex to be deduced from Christian names, the Hollingsworths found not only that mortality was highest among those aged under twenty-five, but also that 'the men were much more affected by plague than the women'. They found also that the general shape of the mortality curve from the plague of 1603 was decidedly downwards from a high level, from probably over 50 per cent for the youngest children to no more than 10 per cent at ages over sixty. Although the age-structure of the population at risk has of necessity to be calculated on the basis of a series of assumptions, the resultant differences in death-rate are of such an order of magnitude that they must reflect the actual effects of plague. As in the Middle Ages, however, seventeenth-century plagues did not invariably exhibit identical characteristics and a more superficial analysis of London plagues after 1603 suggests a considerable measure of diversity. Whereas the 1625 plague in St Botolph's parish 'seems to be probably of the same type' as that of 1603, evidence of the 1605 outbreak in St Margaret's, Westminster, suggests a more uniform spread of victims.

In addition, a large proportion of the other diseases likely to have been prevalent in late medieval England display a preference for young victims, including smallpox, measles, scarlet fever and diphtheria. Moreover, there is evidence that at this time tuberculosis was particularly fatal to adolescents and young adults [22]. Attention has already been drawn to the distorted patterns of age-specific mortality found in Christ Church Priory in the fifteenth century, and extensive calculations from Inquisitions *Post Mortem* have revealed that the death-rates of the under-thirty age-group were disproportionately high in the century and a half after the Black Death [38: *70–5*]. We should note also that the prevalence of diseases which sought out the young relates convincingly to the persistence of negative replacement rates (discussed above pp. 26–9). Finally we can draw further support for our contention from the pulpit. Moralists are always ready to interpret the phenomena of an age, and a later variant on the common theme that plague was a visitation from God to punish man for his sinfulness was that the excessive mortality among children was due to their misbehaviour:

> it may be that [for] vengeaunce of this synne of unwor-schepynge and despysynge of fadres and modres, God sleeth children by pestylence, as ye seeth al day. ffor in the olde lawe children that were rebelle and unbuxom to here fadres and modres were ypunysched by deth, as the fyfthe boke of holy wryt wytnesseth. (Quoted in G. R. Owst, *Literature and Pulpit in Medieval England* [Cambridge, 1933] p. 464.)

It would clearly take some very sophisticated demographic analysis to calculate the precise effects of age- and sex-selective mortality, and the firm data from which such an analysis could be made are unlikely ever to be forthcoming in adequate quantities from medieval sources. But it is clear that if such conditions did exist they would have compounded the impact of the prevailing high level of mortality. Frequent visitations of epidemics which not only killed substantial numbers but also left in their wake distorted age- and/or sex-structures would severely inhibit the ability of the population to reproduce itself. Thus instead of merely a temporary raising of the mortality schedule, the fertility schedule might be lowered for a decade or more as depleted cohorts reached marriageable and child-bearing age.[22] Such an effect would also help to explain the lack of close correlation which sometimes occurred between major outbreaks of plague and economic fluctuations, and which is puzzling to historians.

It is for further research to determine the significance that should be assigned to age- and sex-selective mortality, and the concept remains at present little more than a plausible solution to some of the many perplexing problems posed by the apparent behaviour of population in the later Middle Ages. Nevertheless, the attention of historians should be drawn to the extraordinarily jagged population pyramid of Lichfield in 1695, as presented by Gregory King [27: *182*], and to the recently published study of the demographic history of the Pacific Islands, in which it is argued that age-selective mortality, rather than massive outbreaks of disease, was responsible for the substantial long-term decline in the population of several islands [37].

5 Population in Early Tudor England

THE half century between 1475 and 1525 remains very much a no-man's-land between the main interests of medievalists and early modernists, and it has consequently failed to receive the attention that it merits. Nevertheless both schools of historians have tended to agree that the origins of the demographic explosion of the sixteenth and early seventeenth centuries lay in the last quarter of the century, more especially in the decade 1475 to 1485 [16: *570*; 4: *193*; 24: *44*]. This view would appear to have some truth in it, for at this time, or somewhat earlier, there are the first signs that the long decline in numbers was at last slowing and perhaps even being reversed.

In so far as it is possible to generalise from a wide diversity of regional experience and short-term local ebbs and flows, most economic indicators appear to have reached the bottom of their downward spirals around the middle decades of the fifteenth century. Moreover the direct demographic evidence strongly supports a similar chronology. Replacement rates calculated from Inquisitions *Post Mortem* at last moved above unity after 1445, albeit only marginally and tentatively at first, while those based upon wills show an increase in the numbers of sons surviving their fathers from the 1460s (see above pp. 27–9). But it would be wrong to assume that the population increased rapidly and continuously thereafter, for there are many signs that this early vitality was temporarily undermined some time before the end of the century.

The tendency for the demand for land to quicken in the last quarter of the fifteenth century has been noted in a large number of estate and regional studies, and this quickening has frequently been explained by reference to an expanding population. Such statements as 'the population trend was at last showing marked signs of recovery' [81: *183*] and 'by the 1490s an increasing population deprived the tenants of their ultimate sanction, easy migration' [68: 32] are frequently encountered. The most spectacular increases in rents, both arable and pastoral, are to be found in the counties around London, but evidence of an arresting or reversal of the familiar downward trend is widely based in both England [55: 41–2; 62: 119; 64: 273; 65] and Europe [30: 20–5]. The later fifteenth-century upswing in England's industrial and commercial activity was of even more substantial proportions. The average increase in recorded imports and exports, already rising before the accession of Henry VII, was fully 100 per cent by the accession of Henry VIII twenty-four years later [113]. This remarkable feat was equalled, perhaps even exceeded, by the performance of some major industries [106: 158–9]. The fact that prices did not move decisively before the second decade of the sixteenth century need not preclude a modest increase in population, for the gross under-utilisation of land in the late fifteenth century meant that food production could be increased without difficulty or substantially enhanced costs; while the failure of wage-rates to move upwards in a period of rapidly expanding industrial employment seems to imply an increasing supply of labour, perhaps provided in part by the countryside.

For further indications of the movement of population we can turn to the incidence of disease. Sadly there are no English sources to compare with the German chronicler who was so impressed by the evidence of growth that he wrote in 1483 that 'within these twenty years there has not been any real pestilence; and seldom is there a couple but they have eight, nine, or ten children' [30: 24]. Instead we have only curt references to outbreaks of disease, and the translation of an imperfect epidemiological record into a demographic trend is a most speculative undertaking. Until more research is carried out on the incidence of disease and the level of replacement rates it would be foolish to be dogmatic; none the less there are grounds for believing that the mortality rate may have eased appreciably from time to time in the later fifteenth century. It is possible that the lengthening gaps between major plague outbreaks may have been reflected in some abating of the frequency and virulence of local outbreaks. If one is forced to be specific, the later 1440s and the 1450s and the late 1480s and the 1490s may well have been relatively healthy by the standards of the times.

Yet we must be careful to distinguish any early tentative upward movements in numbers from the well-documented progressive population pressure experienced under the later Tudors and early Stuarts. Evidence is mounting which suggests that in many areas the recovery in the land market was not strong, that it often petered out before 1500, and sometimes went into reverse. It may well prove true that, with the exclusion of those regions benefiting from proximity to London or other expanding food markets, many arable rents did not move sharply upwards before the 1520s [21; 73].[23] Looking to the major towns we find the persistence and, in many cases, the intensification of economic and demographic retrenchment. Judging by the well-documented experience of Coventry, where in the early 1520s a quarter of all the property was vacant and the total population was well on the way to being less than a half of what it had been in 1434 [111: 6–8], we would be ill-advised to dismiss the laments of contemporaries about the decay of England's towns and cities as wild exaggerations.[24] There is more than a grain of truth in such claims as '300 and more dwellings [had] decayed within a few years' before 1487 and 1488 in Gloucester, that 800 ruined houses existed in Bristol in 1518 and over 900 in 1530, and that in 1512 'many and the most partie of all the Cities, Boroughs and Townes corporate wythin this realme of Englande be fallen in ruyn and decaye'.[25]

Nor should the likelihood of an intermittent slackening in the incidence of disease be allowed to create the impression that the closing decades of the fifteenth century and the opening decades of the sixteenth were positively salubrious. The mid-1460s, the early and late 1470s, and the years at the turn of the century saw severe outbreaks of plague in many parts of the country, and in the autumn of 1485 there occurred the first, and by far the most lethal, outbreak of the strange disease known as the English Sweat, which according to chroniclers spread over much of England killing 'young and old and of all manner of ages' in great numbers [47: 230–3, 237–43, 282–8]. It seems probable that these waves of disease temporarily brought to an end or even reversed the tentative recovery.

Yet by the second quarter of the sixteenth century the indications of a marked quickening in population growth become evident. By the 1520s sharp increases had taken place in the prices of foodstuffs, real wages had fallen by a third, and the struggle for land which was to characterise the next hundred years and more was growing in ferocity. By the 1530s contemporaries tell us that the times were less disease-ridden than they had been hitherto, and the earliest series of parish registers, commencing in the 1540s and 1550s, suggest that birth-rates were extremely high.

This is not to say that society was forced against the final limits of subsistence within a short space of time. On the contrary the long decline in population stretching back perhaps almost two hundred years, and the economic contraction of the first three-quarters of the fifteenth century, had created a great deal of slack. Although the testimony of Italian visitors to England on these matters is somewhat suspect owing to the very high density of population in their native lands, it is interesting to learn that a Venetian wrote in the later 1490s that

> Agriculture is not practised in this island beyond what is required for the consumption of the people; because were they to plough and sow all the land that was capable of cultivation, they might sell a quantity of grain to the surrounding countries . . . The population of this island does not appear to me to bear any proportion to her fertility and riches. I rode . . . from Dover to London and from London to Oxford . . . and it seemed to me to be very thinly inhabited; but, lest the way I went . . . should have differed from the other parts of the country, I enquired of those who rode to the north of the kingdom, i.e. to the borders of Scotland, and was told that it was the same case there; nor was there any variety in the report of those who went to Bristol and into Cornwall [137: *10, 31*].

It is also instructive to learn that well-informed English statesmen likewise felt that the country was seriously underpopulated in the 1530s [140: *iii*, *5*]. Indeed the *Dialogue* between Cardinal Pole and Thomas Lupset, as composed by Thomas Starkey, refers at considerable length to the 'grete lake of pepul and skarsenes of men' and to the view that 'in tyme past many mo have byn nurychycd therin, and the cuntrey hath byn more populos, then hyt ys now' [135: *72–6*]. It was claimed that 'batyl and pestylens, hungur and darth' were not the principal causes of this lack of people, rather it was an avoidance of marriage and procreation. Consequently the answer was 'to intyse man to thys lauful maryage and couplyng togydur', and the suggested means of enticement were to repeal the law of chastity in the Church, limit the number of serving men that might be kept, since serving men do not marry, give those who marry a house and a portion of the waste lands at a nominal rent, grant tax reliefs and privileges to those who had five children, and impose a swingeing tax on bachelors [135: *145–52*].

After reading these deliberations one is tempted to speculate that, in order to resist the fall in real wages which followed upon the tendency of the population to increase when the power of disease abated, people were delaying marriage and limiting their families. Such measures, however, could have provided only a palliative, and before 1600 real wages had plunged to the lowest level ever and commentators were increasingly arguing that England was overpopulated [120: *293*].

6 Conclusion

HAVING come this far it is difficult to resist the temptation to engage in the popular sport of guessing at the population of England over the broad sweep of almost half a millennium of history from Domesday to the subsidies of the third decade of the sixteenth century. Domesday Book presents the historical demographer with a set of problems similar to those presented by the 1377 Poll Tax returns. A raw total of about 275,000 persons mentioned in Domesday has to be converted into the national population. Each person is usually taken to be the head of a household, and a multiplier of just under five would appear appropriate to convert them into families. In addition allowance has to be made for four northern counties and at least two major cities omitted from the survey, and for the likelihood of unrecorded sub-tenants and landless men. By these means the 275,000 becomes an estimated 1·75–2·25 million [4: 45; 17: 28–9]. Our next landmark is the Poll Tax, which for reasons outlined above indicates that there were approximately 2·5 to 3 million people in England in 1377 (see p. 14). Our next calculation is extremely speculative, since it involves estimating the loss of population between 1348 and 1377. If we simply add up the death-rates of the four major epidemics between these dates, and assume a static population in the intervening years, then population would have fallen by 65–75 per cent. But to do so would be unrealistic, and substantial allowance must be made for demographic recovery between outbreaks; a net decline of 40–50 per cent might therefore be in order (see above pp. 21–5). If so, England's population in 1348 might well have lain within the range of 4·5 to 6 million, with the balance of possibilities pointing to the higher reaches of this range. Moreover it is unlikely that the population in 1348 was not somewhat lower than it had been at its peak, which was probably around the turn of the thirteenth century.

We move to firmer ground with recent attempts to coax national population figures from the tax returns and muster certificates of the 1520s. As with all pre-census material the use of these records requires considerable judgement; in particular estimates have to be made of the number of people omitted from the tax returns because they were too poor or too young, or from the muster certificates because they were too young or too old. J. Cornwall's resourceful methodology has led him to conclude that the population of England around 1522–5 was of the order of 2·3 million [24]. This figure might well be a little too low since Cornwall, by using Gregory King's age-structure data from the late seventeenth century, a period of relatively low fertility, may well have overestimated the proportion of the population liable to military service. We would thus appear to be justified in suggesting a range of 2·25 to 2·75 million for this date. As we have seen there is good reason to believe that population in the 1520s was somewhat above its lowest point, which was probably reached in the mid-fifteenth century when England may have contained only 2 to 2·5 million people. If this is so then population in the mid-fifteenth century was scarcely, if at all, higher than it had been in 1086, and it had fallen by at least 60 per cent since the Black Death. Furthermore, it is unlikely that the population level of 1377 was exceeded until the second quarter of the sixteenth century.[26] It does not need to be stressed that all these figures are highly speculative, and that the chart of population flows illustrated on p. 71 has even scantier claims to accuracy.

In this account a number of variables have been discussed at some length, including the level of population, the standard of living, the level of economic activity, and the incidence of disease. A plausible attempt can be made to represent graphically the relationship between two of these variables, the level of population and the standard of living, over five centuries of pre-industrial England. Admittedly the population levels portrayed are little more than judicious guesswork and the standard of living is really the real wage-rates of building craftsmen in southern England, but the patterns which they trace in Fig. 2 are in such stark contrast to each other that doubts as to precise accuracy need not be of central importance. It can be seen at a glance that high population coincided with low living standards, and low population with high living standards, and that as population rose so living standards fell, and that as population fell so living standards rose. It can also be seen that in the seven hundred years portrayed by Figs 1 and 2 there were two protracted periods of sharply rising population and two protracted periods of falling, stagnant, or only slowly rising population.

In some respects the relationship that is portrayed between population and real wage-rates could be held to be Malthusian in the long run. Malthusian crises could be postulated for the early fourteenth and mid-seventeenth centuries, and explained in terms of the sharply declining living standards of the preceding eras. Subsequent recoveries in population might be held to have been stimulated by high living standards. Yet it could also be argued that the duration of such cycles, with periods of both rising and falling or stagnant population often exceeding 100 years, was so long as to bring into question whether the relationship between living standards and numbers of people was truly Malthusian. Certainly these time-spans are far removed from the immediacy of the response suggested by Malthus himself and recently by historians, who would portray the demographic experience of pre-industrial Europe in the following terms: 'Whenever in relation to population, land was abundant, birth-rates rose in excess of death-rates and people became more numerous', and 'An amelioration of the conditions of existence, hence of survival, and an increase in economic opportunity had [i.e. before the Industrial Revolution] always been followed by a rise in population'.[27] Likewise the Malthusian checks to a society which appeared gravely to exceed the tolerable limits of existence could be long delayed. The well-known experience of the thirteenth century was repeated in the later sixteenth and early seventeenth centuries, when population continued to rise in the face of a mounting scarcity of food and an appalling slump in living standards.

The lack of a close correlation between living standards and death-rates can be discovered time and again in pre-industrial societies. The Black Death itself struck England after a significant improvement in living standards had taken place, and in the sixteenth century it seems probable that the highest national mortality occurred in the late fifties when living standards still had a long way to fall. It is also noteworthy that the decades of notoriously low living standards at the turn of the sixteenth century were relatively healthy, and that in the later seventeenth and early eighteenth centuries the virulence of successive waves

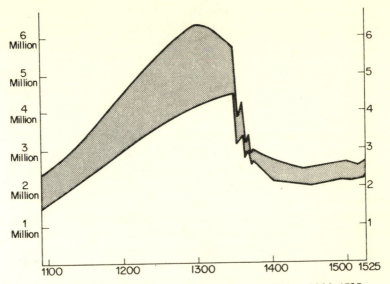

Figure 1: Long-term Flows in English Population, 1086–1525
Showing the Ranges between Plausible Estimates

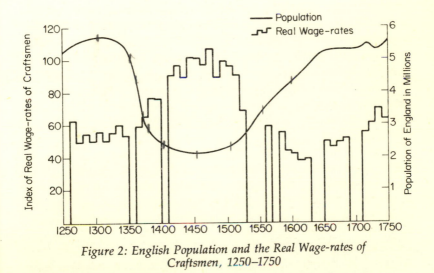

Figure 2: English Population and the Real Wage-rates of
Craftsmen, 1250–1750

The line graph of population is based upon the author's estimates.
The bar graph of real wage-rates is based upon Phelps Brown and Hopkins [125].

of epidemics in England and in Europe bore little relationship to the state of the harvest [23: *87–96*; 34; 42].

Thus evidence drawn from many periods and many parts of pre-industrial Europe confirms the conclusion to be drawn from late medieval England, namely that mortality was not simply a function of the state of the harvest or the level of real wages. This is not to say that there were not innumerable local subsistence crises during which the death-rate rose sharply, for we know that many maladies associated with mainutrition did increase in incidence in times of scarcity; rather that the national population trend was not in the long run invariably determined by such crises. In the long run the major killers were frequently the epidemic and infectious diseases, and these usually varied in incidence according to a wide range of non-economic factors, including the habits of bacteria, fleas, lice, and rats.*

We would conclude therefore that the prime determinant of the course of population in pre-industrial England was mortality rather than fertility, and that changes in real wages were often merely a secondary influence. Yet we would not go so far as to claim that swings in mortality were invariably exogenous. Our understanding of the demographic experience of pre-industrial England may be advanced if we cease to regard mortality as either a Malthusian agent or an exogenous force, and instead acknowledge that these two broad categories of mortality coexisted. The ineluctable logic of the Malthusian cycle, in which mortality is a function of economic change, cannot be overthrown; other things being equal, high living standards did encourage population growth and low living standards did inhibit population growth or bring about decline. But this model is far too simple to cope with the complexities of historical experience: 'other things' frequently did not remain equal. Epidemic and infectious diseases, only distantly if at all related to economic conditions, were a complicating factor, an additional dimension which has to be superimposed upon the basic Malthusian model. In pre-industrial Eng-

*It should be noted that this view is by no means generally accepted. The overwhelming conclusion of the contributors to the Third International Conference of Economic History was that the demographic experience of pre- and early industrial societies was very largely a function of the pace and character of economic change. D. E. C. Eversley (ed.), *Third International Conference of Economic History, Munich, 1965*, Paris (1972). A recent econometric analysis by R. Lee does, however, lend support to the views we have expressed ('Population in Preindustrial England: An Econometric Analysis', *Quarterly Journal of Economics*, LXXVII, 1973).

land the progress of the Malthusian cycle was frequently gravely distorted by epidemic disease. Thus, although population may well have begun to fall, for Malthusian reasons, before 1348, we should not be misled into seeing plague as the inevitable result of dreadful living conditions. Overcrowding and poor sanitation doubtless assisted in the spread of the disease, but there is no reason to suspect that susceptibility to plague is enhanced by malnutrition, and we must entertain the possibility that the second pandemic would have swept through even a prosperous Europe. Certainly it is inconceivable that mortality induced by low living standards could have reduced England's population by more than half and then delayed recovery, despite rising living standards, for almost two centuries. In spite of the protestations of generations of historians there remains much truth in the view that the arrival of plague was a turning-point in history.

Finally we must do something to correct an impression given in this account, and in much of the writing on this period, that living standards can be assessed solely in terms of the amount of goods that a man's wage would purchase. In these terms the fifteenth century was truly the golden age of the English labourer. Yet, as we have seen, these high living standards were not due to any decisive advances in techniques or in the structure of the economy, but to the simple fact that there were fewer people to share the resources of the nation. Moreover, this situation did not result from a once-and-for-all fall in the population, the effects of which have been likened to 'a sort of Marshall Aid on a stupendous scale' for the survivors [2: 91]. Rather, living standards were maintained and improved further by the persistence of very high death-rates which stopped the population from recovering. Clearly an age which relies for its prosperity upon large numbers of its members dying at an early age, and suffering the frequent losses of spouses, children, relatives, friends and colleagues, is somewhat less than golden. Can we wonder that a preoccupation with death and putrefaction is encountered so frequently in the artistic, literary and religious movements of the age [133; 136]? The problems involved in calculating the material well-being of fifteenth-century Englishmen are formidable enough, but those involved in attempting to balance the result against their physical and mental health and their expectation of life are such as to try the skills of even the most imaginative and resourceful of cliometricians. But the impossibility of quantification is no excuse for neglect.

Notes and References

Unless otherwise indicated, London is the place of publication. The abbreviation *E.H.R.* represents *Economic History Review*.

1. Generally sympathetic statements are to be found in W. Abel, *Die Wüstungen des ausgehenden Mittelalters* (Jena, 1943); 'Wüstungen und Preisfall in spätmittelalterlichen Europa', *Jahrbüch für Nationalökonomie und Statistik*, CLXV (1953); J. Schreiner, *Pest og prisfall i senmiddelalderen* (Oslo, 1948); K. F. Helleiner, 'Population Movement and Agrarian Depression in the Later Middle Ages', *Canadian Journal of Economics and Political Science*, LV (1949); and in various contributions to the 'Histoire économique: moyen âge' section of the *Rapports du IXe Congrès international des sciences historiques* (Paris, 1950).

2. For a further statement by Kosminsky, somewhat less sceptical of long-term population decline, see 'Peut-on considérer le xiv et le xv siècles comme l'époque de la décadence de l'économie européenne?' *Studi in onore di Armando Sapori*, 2 vols (Milan, 1957) I, pp. 550–69. The most forceful statement by Kosminsky on this subject, also the earliest, was published in *Voprosi Istorii* in 1948.

3. For general criticisms of Russell's methodology and final estimate, see *Cambridge Economic History of Europe*, vol. I, pp. 561–2; Titow [20: *67–8, 84–5*]; J. Krause, 'The Medieval Household: Large or Small?', *E.H.R.*, 2nd ser., IX (1957). Where local sources exist which permit detailed testing of completeness, the 1377 tax returns are frequently shown to be deficient. For example, S. Thrupp has found that the London returns often omitted apprentices, adolescent children and single women [114: *49–50*]; and M. J. Bennett concludes that a study of a range of complementary sources relating to the clergy in north-west England in the later fourteenth century 'casts doubt upon the high degree of accuracy always claimed for the 1377 returns': 'The Lancashire and Cheshire Clergy, 1379', *Transactions of the Historical Society of Lancashire*

and Cheshire, cxxiv (1973) p. 3. Lesser underenumerations arise from Russell's underestimating the population of Cheshire; see Cornwall [24]; and from his failing to note that the tinners of the south-west were exempt from tax: see J. F. Willard, *Parliamentary Taxes and Personal Property, 1290–1334* (Cambridge, Mass., 1934) pp. 118–20. On the other hand, Russell ascribes the full number of children to the clergy, which is surely taking too literally contemporary complaints of clerical non-celibacy! It is widely appreciated that the first census of 1801 was also seriously defective: Glass and Eversley [27: *223 n. 10*].

4. The data contained in this paragraph differ from those presented by Bean [1: *430, 432–3*] largely because Stone's chronicle [139] has been used to amplify and extend the obituary book.

5. 1361 and 1368 were the peak plague years in London (Creighton [47: *203, 215–16*]; Shrewsbury [53: *126–9, 133–4*]). Some chroniclers reserved the title *pestis tertia* for the outbreak of 1375.

6. Total exports of cloth were as follows: 1359 – 1479 cloths; 1360 – 1550; 1361 – 1496; 1362 – 1144; 1363 – 1544; 1366 – 1931; 1367 – 3219; 1368 – 2756; 1369 – 2497; 1370 – 3181 (Carus-Wilson and Coleman [103: *76–8*]).

7. For generally critical reviews see Morris [51]; P. A. Slack, *English Historical Review*, lxxxvii (1972) 112–15; and R. M. S. McConaghey, *Medical History*, xv (1971) 309–11. The review by P. Laslett in *The Times* (21 February 1971) is much more favourable, and Bridbury [46: *591–2*] finds the arguments of Bean and Shrewsbury concerning the habits and incidence of plague plausible.

8. Far more data, of an admittedly imprecise nature, could be compiled by comparing the numbers of heriots, reliefs, wills, etc., in normal years with those in plague years. This would give widely based indications of the scale of the increase in death-rate, although not of the rate itself.

9. It is significant that the male replacement rates computed by S. Thrupp from later thirteenth-century court rolls are appreciably lower than those recorded from censuses of the same date by H. E. Hallam, 'Some Thirteenth-Century Censuses', *E.H.R.*, 2nd ser., x (1958). Illegitimacy and entry into the Church, further sources of underenumeration, are discussed by Thrupp.

10. The data presented below have been prepared with the assistance of Mr P. Atkinson. The author hopes to publish an article on the demography of the priory.

11. A general study of late medieval towns is sorely needed, but see *inter alia*: Bartlett [100]; E. M. Carus-Wilson, 'The Medieval Trade of the Ports of the Wash', *Medieval Archaeology*, VI–VII (1962–3); *Historic Towns*, ed. M. D. Lobel and E. M. Carus-Wilson (1975) vol. II.

12. Calculated using the formula and figures given in Bridbury [2: 32–3], with adjustments to take account of the changes in the price of wool specified in T. H. Lloyd, *The Movement of Wool Prices in Medieval England*, supplement no. 6 to *E.H.R.* (1973).

13. For critical assessments of valors see: C. D. Ross and T. B. Pugh, 'Materials for the Study of Baronial Incomes in Fifteenth-century England', *E.H.R.*, 2nd ser., VI (1953) 185–94; R. R. Davies, 'Baronial Accounts, Incomes, and Arrears in the Later Middle Ages', *E.H.R.*, 2nd ser., XXI (1968) pp. 213–18. It should also be noted that the structure and purpose of valors differed from estate to estate.

14. Calculated from Table 2, Du Boulay [65: 434]. The calculations were based upon three surviving accounts for the 1450s, seven for the 1460s and five for the 1470s.

15. For example, Bartlett [100]; J. W. F. Hill, *Medieval Lincoln* (Cambridge, 1965) chapter 13; *Bridgewater Borough Archives, 1468–85*, ed. R. W. Dunning and T. D. Tremlett, Somerset Record Society, LXX (1971) pp. xii–xiii; *Historic Towns*, ed. M. D. Lobel (1969) vol. I; *Historic Towns*, ed. M. D. Lobel and E. M. Carus-Wilson (1975) vol. II; and A. F. Butcher's and C. Phythian-Adams's papers on Canterbury and Coventry respectively, presented to the 1971 Urban History Conference at York University, England.

16. It should be noted that the frequently quoted Winchester series of piece-rates for threshing and winnowing understates the rate of increase after 1400. The series has to be based on fewer and fewer manors, for as the fifteenth century progressed demesnes ceased to be cultivated; almost without exception it is the high-wage manors which ceased to be represented. A rate of

around 7·4d. to 7·5d. between 1430 and 1460 would appear to be more accurate representation.

17. The daily wage-rates of building craftsmen and labourers in southern England rose, respectively, from 5d. to 6d. and from 3d. to 4d. in the opening decades of the fifteenth century: Phelps Brown and Hopkins [125]. Rates paid for similar work in Cornwall rose, respectively, from 4d. to 6d. and from 3d. to 4d. in the 1430s: Hatcher [76: *291*].

18. It should be noted, however, that the 20 per cent debasement of 1464 and the subsequent marked upturn in total coinage produced no more than a brief flurry in prices.

19. For a discussion of current thinking concerning fluctuations in pre-industrial populations see Wrigley [43: *62–106*]. It is also instructive to note the similarity between factors used to explain the 'demographic explosion' of the eighteenth and early nineteenth centuries and those ruling in fifteenth-century England. See, for example, Wrigley [43: *146–80*]; H. J. Habakkuk, 'English Population in the Eighteenth Century', *E.H.R.*, 2nd ser., vi (1953); M. Drake (ed.), *Population in Industrialization* (1969).

20. The evidence is slight, but some continental chronicles refer to the frequency of marriages after the Black Death and the Curé of Givry married forty-two couples between 14 January and 24 February 1349, whereas in the previous year he had not conducted a single marriage service: *Cambridge Economic History of Europe*, vol. i, p. 675.

21. On these points see also Creighton [47: *207, 219*] and Shrewsbury [53: *136–8*].

22. The precise effects of distorted sex-structure, and to a lesser extent age-structure, would depend on the proportion of the population which was unmarried. A sizeable reservoir of single persons who subsequently married would help to lessen the impact on fertility. If we accept Hajnal's thesis (above p. 56) then the proportion of single persons of marriageable age was unlikely to have been high; furthermore with a succession of epidemics any reservoir would soon be drained.

23. It must be admitted, however, that rent movements are a poor indication of possible population increase at this time since the lassitude of the preceding era had encouraged many landlords to

grant long leases, and lulled numbers of landlords and tenants into believing that security of tenure at fixed rents and entry fines was the prerogative of all. Time was needed to adjust to changing conditions.

24. In addition to the records and histories of individual towns much of value can be gleaned from John Leland (*The Itinerary of John Leland, 1535–43*, ed. L. Toulmin-Smith, 5 vols., 1907–10), and from Tudor statutes, which list more than fifty cities and towns which had fallen into decay (see in particular the statutes of 4 Henry VII, c. 16; 6 Henry, VIII, c. 5; 7 Henry VIII, c. l; 25 Henry VIII, c. 13; 27 Henry VIII, c. l; 32 Henry VIII, c. 18, 19).

25. W. H. Stevenson, *Calendar of the Records of the Corporation of Gloucester* (1893) no. 59; *Select Cases before the King's Council in the Star Chamber*, ed. I. S. Leadam, Selden Society, xxv (1910) p. 146; G. R. Elton, *Reform and Renewal: Thomas Cromwell and the Common Weal* (Cambridge, 1973) pp. 107–8; *Statutes of the Realm*, 3 Henry VIII, c. 8.

26. Many estimates would have 2·8 to 3 million people in the England of 1500. What is more, since these estimates are based upon the assumption that there were only 2·25 million people in 1377, they imply an *increase* between these two dates of around a third. The thesis that we have outlined runs directly counter to this by arguing for a *decrease* between these dates of around a quarter. Current estimates of the level of population in the early sixteenth century are reviewed in Tucker [41: *209–11*], and Clarkson [3: *25–7*].

27. The quotes are drawn from Y. S. Brenner, *A Short History of Economic Progress* (1969) p. 5, and D. S. Landes, 'Technological Change and Development in Western Europe, 1750–1914', *Cambridge Economic History of Europe*, vol. vi, Pt I (Cambridge, 1965; repr. 1966) p. 274.

Select Bibliography

A comprehensive bibliography of all the topics touched upon in this book would be inordinately long. We have, therefore, provided full details of the sources which have been cited in the text, and for ease of reference these have been arranged in sections, each section being prefaced by brief critical comments. Unless otherwise indicated, London is the place of publication. The abbreviation *E.H.R.* represents *Economic History Review*.

GENERAL STUDIES

All students of the later medieval economy should begin with the works of Postan. Some of his most important studies have been collected together in *Essays on Medieval Agriculture and General Problems of the Medieval Economy* and *Medieval Trade and Finance* (Cambridge, 1973). Saltmarsh's article is also invaluable. Major assaults on the theses of Postan and Saltmarsh have been made by Kosminsky and Bridbury, who dispute that the later Middle Ages experienced a severe depression, and by Bean, who argues that the population decline was probably over by the close of the fourteenth century. Hilton's work places a welcome emphasis on the peasantry, and Du Boulay's on social history.

[1] J. M. W. Bean, 'Plague, Population and Economic Decline in England in the Later Middle Ages', *E.H.R.*, 2nd ser., xv (1963)

[2] A. R. Bridbury, *Economic Growth: England in the Later Middle Ages* (1962).

[3] L. A. Clarkson, *The Pre-Industrial Economy in England, 1500–1750* (1971).

[4] H. C. Darby (ed.), *New Historical Geography of England* (Cambridge, 1973).

[5] F. R. H. Du Boulay, *An Age of Ambition* (1970).

[6] R. H. Hilton, *The English Peasantry in the Later Middle Ages* (Oxford, 1975).

[7] R. H. Hilton, *The Decline of Serfdom in Medieval England* (1969).

[8] E. A. Kosminsky, 'The Evolution of Feudal Rent in England from the XIth to the XVth Centuries', *Past and Present*, 7 (1955).

[9] J. R. Lander, *Conflict and Stability in Fifteenth-Century England* (1970).

[10] E. Miller, 'The English Economy in the Thirteenth Century', *Past and Present*, 28 (1964).

[11] H. A. Miskimin, *The Economy of Early Renaissance Europe, 1300–1460* (Princeton, New Jersey, 1969).

[12] M. M. Postan, 'The Fifteenth Century', *E.H.R..*, ix (1939).

[13] M. M. Postan, 'Some Economic Evidence of Declining Population in the Later Middle Ages,' *E.H.R.*, 2nd ser., ii (1950).

[14] M. M. Postan, 'Histoire économique: moyen âge', *Rapports du IXe congrès international des sciences historiques* (Paris, 1950).

[15] M. M. Postan, 'The Age of Contraction', in *Cambridge Economic History of Europe*, vol. ii (Cambridge, 1952).

[16] M. M. Postan, 'Medieval Agrarian Society in its Prime: England', in *Cambridge Economic History of Europe*, vol. i, 2nd ed. (Cambridge, 1966).

[17] M. M. Postan, *The Medieval Economy and Society: An Economic History of Britain, 1100–1500* (1972).

[18] J. Saltmarsh, 'Plague and Economic Decline in England in the Later Middle Ages', *Cambridge Historical Journal*, vii (1941).

[19] R. S. Schofield, 'The Geographical Distribution of Wealth in England, 1334–1649', *E.H.R.*, 2nd ser., xviii (1965).

[20] J. Z. Titow, *English Rural Society, 1200–1350* (1969).

DEMOGRAPHY

Russell's remarkably resourceful statistical study contains much of great value and remains a standard text, but sadly it has not been revised to take account of the research and debate which have taken place since its publication in 1948. Helleiner has provided a stimulating survey of European developments. Thrupp has introduced ingenious methods for charting population change; Cornwall has attempted to estimate England's population in the 1520s; and Blanchard has gathered evidence from parts of the north and Midlands which indicates the persistence of low levels of population into the sixteenth century. Ohlin has made some perceptive criticisms of work done on medieval demography. Although they deal only in part with the later Middle Ages, the works of Chambers, Hollingsworth (1969) and Wrigley (1969) are highly recommended.

[21] I. Blanchard, 'Population Change, Enclosure and the Early Tudor Economy', *E.H.R.*, 2nd ser., xxiii (1970).

[22] Canterbury Cathedral MS. D 12, Obituary Book of Christ Church Priory.

[23] J. D. Chambers, *Population, Economy, and Society in Pre-Industrial England* (Oxford, 1972).

[24] J. Cornwall, 'English Population in the Early Sixteenth Century', *E.H.R.*, 2nd ser., xxiii (1970).

[25] F. J. Fisher, 'Influenza and Inflation in Tudor England', *E.H.R..*, 2nd ser., xviii (1965).

[26] E. Gautier and L. Henry, *La population de Crulai, paroisse normande* (Paris, 1958).

[27] D. V. Glass and D. E. C. Eversley (eds), *Population in History: Essays in Historical Demography* (1963).

[28] P. Goubert, 'En Beauvaisis: Problèmes démographiques du XVIIIᵉ siècle', *Annales*, vii (1952).

[29] B. F. Harvey, 'The Population Trend in England between 1300 and 1348', *Trans. of the Royal Historical Society*, 5th ser., xvi (1965).

[30] K. Helleiner, 'The Population of Europe from the Black Death to the Eve of the Vital Revolution', in *Cambridge Economic History of Europe*, vol. iv (1967).

[31] M. F. and T. H. Hollingsworth, 'Plague Mortality Rates by Age and Sex in the Parish of St. Botolph's Without Bishopsgate, London, 1603', *Population Studies*, xxv (1971).

[32] T. H. Hollingsworth, 'The Demography of the British Peerage', supplement to *Population Studies*, xviii (1964).

[33] T. H. Hollingsworth, *Historical Demography* (1969).

[34] E. Jutikkala and M. Kauppinen, 'The Structure of Mortality during Catastrophic Years in a Pre-Industrial Society', *Population Studies*, xxv (1971).

[35] R. Lee, 'Population in Preindustrial England: An Econometric Analysis', *Quarterly Journal of Economics*, LXXXVII (1973).

[36] T. R. Malthus, *An Essay on Population*, 2 vols. (1958 edn, ed. M. P. Fogarty).

[37] N. McArthur, *Island Populations of the Pacific* (Canberra, 1968).

[38] G. Ohlin, 'No Safety in Numbers: Some Pitfalls of Historical Statistics', in *Industrialization in Two Systems: Essays in Honor of Alexander Gerschenkron*, ed. H. Rosovsky (New York, 1966).

[39] J. C. Russell, *British Medieval Population* (Albuquerque, 1948).

[40] S. Thrupp, 'The Problem of Replacement Rates in Late Medieval English Population', *E.H.R.*, 2nd ser., XVIII (1965).

[41] G. S. L. Tucker, 'English Pre-Industrial Population Trends', *E.H.R.*, 2nd ser., XVI (1963).

[42] G. Utterström, 'Some Population Problems in Pre-Industrial Sweden', *Scandinavian Economic History Review*, II (1954).

[43] E. A. Wrigley, *Population and History* (1969).

[44] E. A. Wrigley, 'Family Limitation in Pre-Industrial England', *E.H.R.*, 2nd ser., XIX (1966).

[45] E. A. Wrigley, 'Mortality in Pre-Industrial England: The Example of Colyton, Devon, over Three Centuries', *Daedalus*, 97 (1968).

DISEASE

The standard works on the medical aspects of plague are by Hurst and Pollitzer. Creighton's book, despite errors on medical matters, is still a useful guide. Shrewsbury's book also contains much of value, although many of its conclusions are extremely controversial; Morris's review essay should be read as a corrective. Ziegler has provided a good readable introduction to the first outbreak of plague.

√[46] A. R. Bridbury, 'The Black Death', *E.H.R.*, 2nd ser., XXVI (1973).

√[47] C. Creighton, *A History of Epidemics in England* (1965 edn) I.

[48] J. L. Fisher, 'The Black Death in Essex', *Essex Review*, LII (1943).

[49] L. F. Hirst, *The Conquest of Plague: A Study of the Evolution of Epidemiology* (Oxford, 1953).

[50] W. MacArthur, 'The Identification of Some Pestilences Recorded in the Irish Annals', *Irish Historical Studies*, VI (1948–9).

[51] C. Morris, 'The Plague in Britain', *Historical Journal*, XIV (1971).

[52] R. Pollitzer, *Plague* (Geneva, 1954).

[53] J. F. D. Shrewsbury, *The History of Bubonic Plague in England* (Cambridge, 1970).

[54] P. Ziegler, *The Black Death* (1969).

THE ECONOMY

The vast bulk of our knowledge of late medieval economic developments is contained in the studies of particular manors, estates, towns, industries, trades, and regions, some of which are listed below. For an overview see, in addition to the works listed in the first section, the works of Duby, Carus-Wilson (1967), Carus-Wilson and Coleman, and Power and Postan (eds).

Agriculture and Agrarian Society

[55] J. M. W. Bean, *The Estates of the Percy Family, 1416–1557* (Oxford, 1958).

[56] M. W. Beresford and J. G. Hurst (eds), *Deserted Medieval Villages* (1971).

[57] J. R. Birrell, 'The Honour of Tutbury in the Fourteenth and Fifteenth Centuries', Birmingham University M.A. thesis (1962).

[58] I. S. W. Blanchard, 'Economic Change in Derbyshire in the Later Middle Ages, 1272–1540', London University Ph.D. thesis (1967).

[59] P. F. Brandon, 'Arable Farming in a Sussex Scarp-foot Parish during the Late Middle Ages', *Sussex Archaeological Collections*, C (1962).

[60] P. F. Brandon, 'The Common Lands and Wastes of Sussex', London University Ph.D. thesis (1963).

[61] J. A. Brent, 'Alciston Manor in the Later Middle Ages', *Sussex Archaeological Collections*, cvi (1968).

[62] M. N. Carlin, 'Christ Church, Canterbury, and its Lands, from the Beginning of the Priorate of Thomas Chillenden to the Dissolution, 1391–1450', Oxford University B.Litt. thesis (1970).

[63] E. B. DeWindt, *Land and People in Holywell-cum-Needingworth: Structures of Tenure and Patterns of Social Organization in an East Midlands Village, 1252–1457* (Toronto, 1972).

[64] R. B. Dobson, *Durham Priory, 1400–1450* (Cambridge, 1973).

[65] F. R. H. Du Boulay, 'A Rentier Economy in the Later Middle Ages: The Archbishopric of Canterbury', *E.H.R.*, 2nd ser., xvi (1964).

[66] F. R. H. Du Boulay, *The Lordship of Canterbury: An Essay on Medieval Society* (1966).

[67] G. Duby, *Rural Economy and Country Life in the Medieval West* (1968 edn).

[68] C. Dyer, 'A Redistribution of Incomes in Fifteenth-Century England?', *Past and Present*, 39 (1968).

[69] R. J. Faith, 'The Peasant Land Market in Berkshire', Leicester University Ph.D. thesis (1962).

[70] H. P. R. Finberg, *Tavistock Abbey: A Study in the Social and Economic History of Devon* (Cambridge, 1951).

[71] H. S. A. Fox, 'The Chronology of Enclosure and Economic Development in Medieval Devon', *E.H.R.*, 2nd ser., xxviii (1975).

[72] H. E. Hallam, 'The Agrarian Economy of South Lincolnshire in the Mid-Fifteenth Century', *Nottingham Medieval Studies*, xi (1967).

[73] B. J. Harris, 'Landlords and Tenants in the Later Middle Ages: The Buckingham Estates', *Past and Present*, 43 (1969).

[74] B. F. Harvey, 'The Leasing of the Abbot of Westminster's Demesnes in the Later Middle Ages', *E.H.R.*, 2nd ser., xxii (1969).

[75] P. D. A. Harvey, *A Medieval Oxfordshire Village: Cuxham, 1240–1400* (Oxford, 1965).

[76] J. Hatcher, *Rural Economy and Society in the Duchy of Cornwall, 1300–1500* (Cambridge, 1970).

[77] R. H. Hilton, *The Economic Development of Some Leicester-shire Estates in the Fourteenth and Fifteenth Centuries* (Oxford, 1947).

[78] D. J. B. Hindley, 'The Economy and Administration of the Estates of the Dean and Chapter of Exeter Cathedral in the Fifteenth Century,' Exeter University M.A. thesis (1958).

[79] G. A. Holmes, *The Estates of the Higher Nobility in Four-teenth-century England* (Cambridge, 1957).

[80] R. I. Jack (ed.), *The Grey of Ruthin Valor: The Valor of the English Lands of Edmund Grey, Earl of Kent, drawn up from Ministers' Accounts of 1467–68* (Sydney, 1965).

[81] I. Kershaw, *Bolton Priory: The Economy of a Northern Monas-tery, 1286–1325* (Oxford, 1973).

[82] J. L. Kirby, 'The Hungerford Family in the Later Middle Ages', London M.A. thesis (1939).

[83] A. E. Levett and A. Ballard, 'The Black Death on the Estates of the See of Winchester', in *Oxford Studies in Social and Legal History*, vol. v. (Oxford, 1916).

[84] R. P. McKinley, *Norfolk Surnames in the Sixteenth Century*, Leicester University Department of English Local History, Occasional Papers, 2nd ser., ii (Leicester, 1969).

[85] F. M. Page, *The Estates of Crowland Abbey* (Cambridge, 1934).

[86] R. C. Payne, 'The Agricultural Estates in Wiltshire of the Duchy of Lancaster in the 13th, 14th, and 15th Centuries', London University Ph.D. thesis (1939).

[87] A. J. Pollard, 'Estate Management in the Later Middle Ages: The Talbots and Whitchurch, 1383–1525', *E.H.R.*, 2nd ser., xxv (1972).

[88] J. A. Raftis, *The Estates of Ramsey Abbey: A Study in Economic Growth and Organization* (Toronto, 1957).

[89] J. A. Raftis, *Warboys: Two Hundred Years in the Life of an English Medieval Village* (Toronto, 1974).

[90] A. F. Roderick, 'Agrarian Conditions in Herefordshire and the Adjacent Border during the Later Middle Ages', London University Ph.D. thesis (1938).

[91] E. Searle, *Lordship and Community: Battle Abbey and its Banlieu, 1066–1538* (Toronto, 1974).

[92] B. H. Slicher Van Bath, *The Agrarian History of Western Europe, A.D. 500–1850* (1963).

[93] R. A. L. Smith, *Canterbury Cathedral Priory: A Study in Monastic Administration* (Cambridge, 1943).

[94] R. Somerville, *The Duchy of Lancaster, 1265–1603* (1953).

[95] R. L. Storey, *Thomas Langley and the Bishopric of Durham* (1961).

[96] J. Z. Titow, 'Some Differences between Manors and their Effects on the Condition of the Peasants in the Thirteen Century,' *Agricultural History Review*, x (1962).

[97] G. H. Tupling, *The Economic History of Rossendale*, Chetham Society, new ser., LXXXVI (Manchester, 1927).

[98] *Victoria County History: Hampshire*, vol. v (1912).

[99] *Victoria County History: Wiltshire*, vol. iv (1959).

Industry, Towns and Trade

[100] J. N. Bartlett, 'The Expansion and Decline of York in the Later Middle Ages', *E.H.R.*, 2nd ser., xii (1959).

[101] E. M. Carus-Wilson, *Medieval Merchant Venturers* (1967 edn).

[102] E. M. Carus-Wilson, 'Evidences of Industrial Growth on some Fifteenth-Century Manors', *E.H.R.*, 2nd ser., xii (1959).

[103] E. M. Carus-Wilson and O. Coleman, *England's Export Trade, 1275–1547* (Oxford, 1963).

[104] O. Coleman, 'Trade and Prosperity in the Fifteenth Century: Some Aspects of the Trade of Southampton', *E.H.R.*, 2nd ser., xvi (1963).

[105] N. S. B. Gras, *The Evolution of the English Corn Market from the Twelfth to the Eighteenth Century* (New York, 1967 edn).

[106] J. Hatcher, *English Tin Production and Trade before 1550* (Oxford, 1973).

[107] J. Hatcher and T. C. Barker, *A History of British Pewter* (1974).

✗ [108] H. Heaton, *The Yorkshire Woollen and Worsted Industries* (Oxford, 1920).

[109] M. K. James, *Studies in the Medieval Wine Trade* (Oxford, 1971).

[110] B. McClennaghan, *The Springs of Lavenham* (Ipswich, 1924).

[111] C. Phythian-Adams, 'Coventry and the Problem of Urban

Decay in the Later Middle Ages' (unpublished paper submitted to the 1971 Urban History Conference).

[112] E. Power and M. M. Postan (eds), *Studies in English Trade in the Fifteenth Century* (1933).

[113] P. Ramsey, 'Overseas Trade in the Reign of Henry VII: The Evidence of the Customs Accounts', *E.H.R.*, 2nd ser., VI (1953).

[114] S. Thrupp, *The Merchant Class of Medieval London* (Ann Arbor, Michigan, 1962).

WAGES, PRICES AND MONEY SUPPLY

The articles by Phelps Brown and Hopkins provide the best introduction. Thorold Rogers remains, after more than a century, the fount of most data, with Beveridge's articles providing a valuable supplement. Miskimin, Robinson, and Shreiner emphasise the importance of money supply in creating the economic conditions of the later Middle Ages, while Postan and Cipolla minimise it.

[115] W. H. Beveridge, 'The Yield and Price of Corn in the Middle Ages', *Economic History*, II (1927).

[116] W. H. Beveridge, 'A Statistical Crime of the Seventeenth Century', *Journal of Economic and Business History*, I (1929).

[117] W. H. Beveridge, 'Wages in the Winchester Manors', *E.H.R.*, VII (1936).

[118] W. H. Beveridge, 'Westminster Wages in the Manorial Era', *E.H.R.*, 2nd ser., VIII (1955).

[119] C. Cipolla, 'Currency Depreciation in Medieval Europe', *E.H.R.*, 2nd ser., XV (1963).

[120] D. C. Coleman, 'Labour in the English Economy of the Seventeenth Century', *E.H.R.*, 2nd ser., VIII (1956).

[121] Sir John Craig, *The Mint: A History of the London Mint from A.D. 287 to 1948* (Cambridge, 1953).

[122] M. Friedman, 'The Supply of Money and Changes in Prices and Output', in *The Controversy over the Quantity Theory of Money*, ed. E. Dean (Boston, Mass., 1965).

[123] H. A. Miskimin, 'Monetary Movements and Market Structure, Forces for Contraction in Fourteenth and Fifteenth Century England', *Journal of Economic History*, XXIV (1964).

[124] E. H. Phelps Brown and S. V. Hopkins, 'Seven Centuries of Building Wages', *Economica* (1955).

[125] E. H. Phelps Brown and S. V. Hopkins, 'Seven Centuries of the Prices of Consumables, Compared with Builders' Wage-Rates', *Economica* (1956). Both [124] and [125] are reprinted in E. M. Carus-Wilson (ed.), *Essays in Economic History*, vol. ii (1962).

[126] M. M. Postan, 'Note', *E.H.R.*, 2nd ser., xii (1959).

[127] ✳ W. C. Robinson, 'Money, Population and Economic Change in Late Medieval Europe', *E.H.R.*, 2nd ser., xii (1959).

[128] J. Thorold Rogers, *A History of Agriculture and Prices in England*, 7 vols (Oxford, 1866–1902).

[129] J. Schreiner, 'Wages and Prices in England in the Later Middle Ages', *Scandinavian Economic History Review*, ii (1954).

CONTEMPORARY COMMENT AND SOCIAL DEVELOPMENTS

Medieval chronicles are an important source of information on outbreaks of disease, but they rarely refer in detail to economic and social matters. By the later fifteenth and the early sixteenth centuries, however, contemporaries were commenting much more extensively on such matters, and the *Italian Relation* [137] and Thomas Starkey [135] are good examples of this welcome development. Huizinga and Crawfurd stress the impact of recurrent waves of disease on artistic and social attitudes.

[130] F. E. Baldwin, *Sumptuary Legislation and Personal Regulation in England* (Baltimore, 1926).

[131] *Chronicon Adae de Usk, A.D. 1377–1421*, ed. E. M. Thomson (Oxford, 1904).

[132] G. G. Coulton, *Medieval Panorama* (Cambridge, 1945).

[133] R. Crawfurd, *Plague and Pestilence in Literature and Art* (Oxford, 1914).

[134] G. R. Elton, *England 1200–1640* (1969).

[135] *England in the Reign of King Henry the Eighth*, ed. S. J. Herrtage, Early English Text Society, extra ser., xxxii (1878).

[136] J. Huizinga, *The Waning of the Middle Ages* (1955 edn).

[137] *Italian Relation of England: A Relation or rather a True Account*

of the Island of England, ed. C. A. Sneyd, Camden Society, XXXVII (1847).

[138]   *Polychronicon Ranulphi Higden, Monachi Cestrensis*, ed. C. Babington and J. R. Lumby, 9 vols, Rolls Ser. (1865–96).

[139]   W. G. Searle (ed.), *The Chronicle of John Stone, Monk of Christ Church, 1415–71*, Cambridge Antiquarian Society, XXXIV (Cambridge, 1902).

[140]   *Tudor Economic Documents*, ed. R. H. Tawney and E. Power, 3 vols (1924).

[141]   Thomas Walsingham, *Historia Anglicana*, ed. H. T. Riley, 2 vols, Rolls Ser. (1836–4).

Index

Adam of Usk   16, 59
agriculture, fortunes of   31–3, 35–43, 63–5
Anonimalle Chronicle   16, 58

Battle Abbey estates   39
Bean, J. M. W.   15, 16–18, 19
Berkshire   39
Birmingham   46
Bishop's Waltham   22
Black Death   19, 21–5; *see also* plague
Bolton Priory estates   37
Boston   34
Bradford   46
Bridbury, A. R.   15, 36
Brightwell   22
Bristol   34, 65

Cambridgeshire   22, 38
Canterbury   17; cathedral   40; archbishopric estates   41; *see also* Christ Church Priory
Castle Combe   46
Chambers, J. D.   15
Cheshire   37
Christ Church Priory, Canterbury: demographic data   17–18, 29–30; estates   32, 40–1
clergy, mortality of   17–18, 21–2, 23–5
cloth exports   18, 34, 76; industry   34, 45–7
Coggeshall   46
Colchester   45
Colyton   56
Cornwall   22, 42, 46, 48
Cornwall, J.   20, 69
court rolls   28–9, 43–4

Coventry   34, 65
Creighton, C.   16
Crowland Abbey estates   38
Cumberland   37
Cuxham   22

De Chauliac, Guy   59
demand, patterns of   33–5, 45–6, 50
Denbighshire   32
Derbyshire   32, 37–8
Devon   42, 46
DeWindt, E. A.   44
disease, and living standards   11–12, 69–73
diseases (other than plague)   11–12, 18–19, 57–8, 60–1, 62, 65; *see also* epidemics, mortality, plague
Domesday Book, population estimate from   68
Dorset   32
Downton   22
Du Boulay, F. R. H.   15, 41
Duby, G.   15, 56
Duchy of Lancaster estates   32, 37, 39
Durham, bishopric estates   37
Durham Priory estates   37
dysentery   58

East Anglia   25, 32
epidemics: 1348–9 *see* Black Death; 1360–2   18, 25, 58–9; 1368–9   18, 25, 59; 1390–1   59; 1400   59; 1420   57; 1427   57–8; 1457–8   58; 1485   58, 65; *see also* diseases, plague, 'Sweat', *mure*, typhus

Plymouth 45
Poll Tax, returns of 1377 13–14, 46, 56, 68, 75–6
Pollitzer, R. 59
Postan, M. M. 12, 36, 47, 57
prices 47–54, 64, 65, 78

Raftis, J. A. 44
Ramsey Abbey estates 32, 38
Reading 45
replacement rates 14, 26–9, 63
Rogers, J. T. 49
Russell, J. C. 12, 13–15, 25–6

St Botolph's parish, London 60
Salisbury 45
Saltmarsh, J. 12, 15
Schreiner, J. 15
Scotland 57
Shrewsbury, J. F. D. 18–19, 25
Shropshire 37
Smith, R. A. L. 40
Somerset 32, 39, 46
Southampton 34
Staffordshire 32, 37–8, 46
Starkey, Thomas 66–7
Statutes of Labourers 48
Stroudwater 46
Sudbury 46
Suffolk 46
Surrey 46
Sussex 39, 48
'Sweat', the 18, 58, 65

tenants-in-chief: mortality of 22,

23–4, 25–6, 61; replacement rates of 26–8, 63
Thrupp, S. 28–9, 56
tin, production 34–5
Titow, J. Z. 56–7
Tiverton 46
Totnes 46
towns, fortunes of 34–5, 44–5, 46, 65
tuberculosis 58, 61
typhus 19, 58

wage-rates 11, 36, 47–54, 64, 65, 67, 69, 77–8
Wakefield 46
Walsingham, Thomas 16, 59
Warboys 44
Warwickshire 38
Westminster 49, 51; St Margaret's parish 60
Westminster Abbey estates 38, 49
wills 17, 28–9, 63
Wiltshire 39, 42
Winchester, bishopric estates 32, 39, 48, 51
wine imports 35, 36
Witney 22
wool exports 34–5
Worcester 45
Worcestershire 38, 46
Wrigley, E. A. 15, 19–20, 56

York 34; diocese 22
Yorkshire 37

NOV 0 1 1978